Laugh Lines

LAUGH LINES

Humor, Genre, and Political Critique in Late Twentieth-Century American Poetry

CARRIE CONNERS

University Press of Mississippi / Jackson

The University Press of Mississippi is the scholarly publishing agency of
the Mississippi Institutions of Higher Learning: Alcorn State University,
Delta State University, Jackson State University, Mississippi State University,
Mississippi University for Women, Mississippi Valley State University,
University of Mississippi, and University of Southern Mississippi.

www.upress.state.ms.us

The University Press of Mississippi is a member
of the Association of University Presses.

Copyright © 2022 by University Press of Mississippi
All rights reserved

An earlier condensed version of chapter 2 appeared in *Reading the Difficulties: Dialogues with Contemporary American Innovative Poetry*, edited by Thomas Fink and Judith Halden-Sullivan (University of Alabama Press, 2014).

An earlier condensed version of chapter 3 appeared in *The Changing Image of the Businessman through Literature*, edited by Christa Mahalik (Cambridge Scholars Press, 2010).

First printing 2022

∞

Library of Congress Cataloging-in-Publication Data

Names: Conners, Carrie, author.
Title: Laugh lines : humor, genre, and political critique in late twentieth-century American poetry / Carrie Conners.
Description: Jackson : University Press of Mississippi, 2022. | Includes bibliographical references and index.
Identifiers: LCCN 2021061688 (print) | LCCN 2021061689 (ebook) | ISBN 9781496839534 (hardback) | ISBN 9781496839527 (trade paperback) | ISBN 9781496839503 (epub) | ISBN 9781496839510 (epub) | ISBN 9781496839480 (pdf) | ISBN 9781496839497 (pdf)
Subjects: LCSH: Humorous poetry, American—History and criticism. | American wit and humor—History and criticism. | American poetry—20th century—History and criticism.
Classification: LCC PS309.H85 C66 2022 (print) | LCC PS309.H85 (ebook) | DDC 811/.0709054—dc23/eng/20220209
LC record available at https://lccn.loc.gov/2021061688
LC ebook record available at https://lccn.loc.gov/2021061689

British Library Cataloging-in-Publication Data available

for Fred

Contents

ix   Acknowledgments

3   Introduction

19   **CHAPTER ONE** | The Good Life
       The Politics of Hedonism in Marilyn Hacker's *Love, Death, and the Changing of the Seasons*

45   **CHAPTER TWO** | Bursting at the Seams
       Exploding the Confines of Reification with Creative Constraints in Harryette Mullen's *Sleeping with the Dictionary*

79   **CHAPTER THREE** | "But He Aint Never Been Seen!"
       The Protean Howard Hughes and Overlapping Capitalist Narratives in Ed Dorn's *Gunslinger*

105   **CHAPTER FOUR** | Russell Edson's Bestiary
       Humanists in a Posthuman World

137   **CODA** | Connections and Conclusions

143   Notes

149   Works Cited

155   Index

Acknowledgments

I'd like to thank Lynn Keller for her invaluable assistance with this project, as well as her guidance, both professional and personal, through all of the stages of my career. No matter how many other commitments she had, she has always taken the time to comment on drafts, talk through ideas, assuage my anxieties, and answer my many, many questions. She is a model of professional kindness whom I seek to emulate. I'd also like to thank Ron Wallace, Tom Schaub, Heather Dubrow, and Tracy Curtis who have generously given their time to support this project and provided helpful suggestions since the early stages; for these efforts I am grateful. I'd also like to thank Jesse Lee Kercheval, Cyrena Pondrom, Amy Quan Barry, Rob Nixon, Jeff Steele, and Rebecca Walkowitz for sharing with me their knowledge of teaching, writing, and their respective fields. A special mention is required for Robyn Shanahan, who helped me navigate bureaucratic challenges with good humor and kindness. I'd be remiss without thanking Steve Carr and Jan Beatty.

To my writing group members, past and present—John Bradley, Rob Henn, Samaa Abdurraqib, Xochitl Gilkeson, Laura Tanenbaum, and Sara Philips—I owe more than I can give. Their friendship, patience, brilliant suggestions, camaraderie, and laughter have made the experience of writing gratifying and enjoyable. Many of the ideas in this project were developed with them. I owe thanks to my FFPP Writing Group: Christopher Schmidt, Matt Brim, Lesley Broder, Andras Kisery, and Tshombe Walker, led by the inimitable Shelley Eversley. Their feedback was critical in the revision of this manuscript. PSC-CUNY supported the revision of this project through a PSC-CUNY grant for which I am grateful. Thanks to Tom Fink and Judith Halden-Sullivan for including a version of chapter 2 in their wonderful volume *Reading the Difficulties: Dialogues with Contemporary American Innovative Poetry.*

In addition to these people and organizations, I'd like to thank my dear friends Lauren Vedal, Brian O'Camb, Annette Vee, Mike Shapiro, Nmachi Nwokebia, Sonia Alejandra Rodríguez, Jayashree Kamble, Natalie Havlin, Meghan Fox, Hara Bastas, Kristen Gallagher, and Jackie Jones for their sparkling conversation and steady compassion.

I am forever grateful for the company of my writing buddy Jeeves, the late, great, willful basset hound, who both served as an audience for what would have been raving soliloquies about difficult ideas and forced me to drop the books and tear myself away from the computer screen to go outside once in a while.

My family, especially my parents Paula and Jerry Conners and my brother Chris Conners, has been enthusiastically, unconditionally supportive of everything I have done, which I appreciate enormously. I thank Amanda Cleaver, my best woman, my sister, for putting up with me and always being there. And finally, and most heartily, I thank my husband Fred for his limitless patience, his helpful suggestions, his sense of humor, and his unyielding support and love.

Laugh Lines

Introduction

Several writers have remarked upon the relationship between poetry and humor. Henri Bergson, an influential humor theorist, claims in his famous piece "Laughter: An Essay on the Meaning of the Comic" that "In every wit there is something of a poet" (50). Howard Nemerov suggests that poetry and jokes share similar characteristics and structures including "limited material," surprising resolution of "apparent absurdity," and a revelation of deeper meaning (11). In addition to these shared characteristics, poetry and jokes, Nemerov claims, involve an element of rebellion (12). Humor disrupts order, whether imposed or received, which creates sites of rupture in language and in thought. These ruptured sites invite investigation, curiosity, and critique, creating ample opportunity for social criticism and political inquiry. Humor, as Freud argues, serves as an outlet for repression and destabilizes ideas. Applied to poetry, Freud's ideas suggest that humor can enable poets to communicate viewpoints that contradict those of a conservative establishment. I argue that humor is integral to the character of contemporary American poetry, and that, in order to achieve a more comprehensive understanding of that poetry, we must take a closer look at its humor.[1] Although more scholarship on the role of humor in American poetry in general is needed, this book by necessity is narrower in scope. It investigates a selection of politically engaged contemporary American poetry written between the 1960s and 2001 in varied poetic genres for which humor is not just an aesthetic feature, but a source of critique concerning American society, including, importantly, its language. I argue that the interplay between humor and poetic genre creates special opportunities for political critique as poetic genres invoke the social constructs that the poets deride.

Though critics have long recognized the use of humor in poetry to critique and satirize societies, the strong trend toward humorous social and political critique in American poetry since the end of World War II has been largely overlooked. There are some important exceptions, such as the sixth and seventh chapters of Ron Wallace's *God Be with the Clown: Humor in American Poetry*; *Humor in Modern American Poetry*, a collection of essays published in 2018 which focuses on modern American poetry, not contemporary American poetry, and analyzes "poets born no later than 1928," a date after which all of the poets in this study were born (Trousdale 12);[2] a recent special issue of *Humor: International Journal of Humor Research*, focused on humor in contemporary American poetry and edited by Denise Duhamel, a poet known for the use of humor in her work, and Salvatore Attardo, a humor theorist; and Calista McRae's *Lyric as Comedy: The Poetics of Abjection in Postwar America*, which links the "solipsistic, self-dramatizing, self-distancing procedures of stand-up" comedy to the presentation of the self in American mid-twentieth century and twenty-first century lyric poetry (McRae). McRae's insightful book excludes the poetic genres of most of the poetry analyzed in this study.[3] Two recent poetry anthologies highlight humorous American poetry. Charles Harper Webb edited an anthology titled *Stand Up Poetry* that showcases humorous poetry, but Webb's definition of "stand up poetry" in his introduction is rather limiting, focusing on accessible poetry, excluding difficult or experimental poetry that employs humor. Barbara Hamby and David Kirby edited another collection of humorous poetry *Seriously Funny*, but again focus on accessible poetry. Neither anthology introduction substantially links poetic humor to sociopolitical critique or discusses the interplay of humor and the conventions of poetic genre. In their introduction to the special issue of *Humor* mentioned above, Duhamel and Attardo lament the dearth of scholarship that addresses the topic. And, at the end of the introduction to *Humor in Modern American Poetry*, Rachel Trousdale calls for scholars to join the conversation about humor in poetry, specifically noting the need for more scholarship on humor in contemporary poetry (15). This book seeks to contribute to this burgeoning conversation.

This trend toward humorous sociopolitical critique in American poetry written after World War II appears to have been prompted by several factors that helped to shape the political climate, including the repression of dissent in the 1950s, due in part to McCarthyism and to the awareness of vulnerability to the destructive power of atomic energy. The restrictive climate of literary studies in the immediate post-war years, dominated by the New Critical ideals that valued poems as autonomous art objects rather than products of a particular social and political context, also contributed to the increasing number of poets whose work rebelliously deployed humor to engage with politics. For example, in work like *Howl and Other Poems* (1956), Allen Ginsberg exploded forms and expectations with exuberant, often crass, celebrations and laments filled with humor. As numerous poets and critics have argued, within a particular historical moment, the form of a poem may be a political decision in its own right; certainly, contemporary poets' experiments and engagements with form contribute to both humor and political critique, often serving as the source for both. I analyze how selected US poets writing from the later decades of the twentieth century to the turn of the twenty-first century (from the 1960s through 2001) have strategically used humor to combat and critique societal and literary norms.

Through my research I have observed that humorous political poetry of this time period differs from that of earlier decades because of the changes in American culture and historical events, especially the Vietnam War and the counterculture associated with resistance to the war, disillusionment with late capitalism, and civil rights movements that fought for the rights of women, racial minorities, and the LGBTQI community. As Trousdale notes in the Introduction to *Humor in Modern American Poetry*, modern poetry—that written in the in the first half of the twentieth century—has a reputation of being difficult, demanding of the reader, efficient, precise, and serious (1). Because of these conceptions, and because of modernist poetry's tendencies toward objectivity and impersonality that much of contemporary poetry consciously departs from, the humor in modern poetry and the critical conversation about it differ from the humor in and the conversations about contemporary poetry.

I chose to exclude twenty-first century humorous political poetry because of the marked shift in the political climate that occurred after September 11, 2001. As Philip Metres observes in *Behind the Lines: War Resistance Poetry on the American Homefront since 1941*,

> the representation of the terrorist attacks momentarily opened a gap in the national self-definition, as the word "empire" now became visible as part of the discourse.... The use of this term in much of the mainstream discussion did not imply a reconsideration of the imperial adventures during and after the Cold War that arguably fostered the attacks on the World Trade Center and the Pentagon on that dark day. Rather, the US administration officials implicitly embraced the new thinking, coining War on Terror as war in which nations would be either with us or against us in the search for Operation Infinite Justice. The War on Terror, then, became the latest brand name for Pure War—both in its furthering of the national security state at home and in its policy of preemptive strikes on "states that sponsor terrorism." In other words, the terms of critique employed by the Left—"empire" and "Pure War"—now became visible and justifiable in light of the terrorist attacks. (220)

The attacks and the radical shift in the political climate, in particular the rhetoric Metres describes above, inspired a great deal of political poetry. However, because the poetry produced reflects the swift cultural changes that occurred after September 11, 2001, it merits its own study.

In addition to political climate, and probably in part because of it, post–World War II America witnessed numerous groundbreaking, politically charged comics. Moreover, multiple influential cultural events and theories emerged in which humor played an important role. Near the beginning of the time period, Lenny Bruce pushed censorship boundaries, which, in turn, influenced others, such as George Carlin. Carlin vehemently criticized censorship in his famous bit, "Seven Words You Can Never Say on Television," which played a role in a Supreme Court case on censorship: "Shit, piss, fuck, cunt, cocksucker, motherfucker, and tits. Those are the heavy seven. Those are the ones that'll infect your soul, curve your spine, and keep the country from winning the war" (*Class Clown*). Richard Pryor's brilliant and vulgar stand-up routines boldly addressed racial issues. Lily Tomlin blurred gender roles and Roseanne Barr, the crass "domestic goddess," to use her term, revealed the unglamorous aspects of life as a working-class woman. Woody Allen, Whoopi Goldberg, Eddie Murphy, Jon Stewart, Chris Rock, and Margaret Cho also emerged as influential comics whose routines addressed important cultural issues. Television comedy shows such as *Saturday Night Live*, *In Living Color*, *The Simpsons*, and *South Park* featured political and social satire. Herbert Marcuse's theory of "play" influenced thinkers, and Abbie Hoffman inspired legions of Vietnam War protestors through his comical, theatrical demonstrations. Poets, like the rest of American citizens, were aware of these people, programs, events, and ideas permeating their culture, and undoubtedly many were influenced or inspired by them.

Though such poets as Frank O'Hara, Heather McHugh, Denise Duhamel, Tony Hoagland, Dean Young, James Tate, and Charles Bukowski are known for the humor in their work during the same time period as this study—the 1960s through 2001—much of the humor in late twentieth-century American poetry has been ignored by critics or treated as a relatively minor feature of the work, not as essential to the work's purpose. In contrast, criticism focused on American fiction from the same time period, especially that classified as "postmodern" or "metafiction," has been much more engaged with the importance of humor and its relationship to politics in texts, often discussing humor as a major component of the work that facilitates the complication of meanings, the destabilization of received categories, etc. Why, then, has contemporary American poetry not been considered in the same light?

One plausible potential response to that question is that the reverence for the traditionally lofty genre of lyric interferes with recognition of humor. Virginia Jackson in her article "Who Reads Poetry?" discusses the consequences of the all-too-common association of all genres of poetry with the lyric, which, she claims, in recent years came to be defined as "a short, nonnarrative poem depicting the subjective experience of a speaker":

> the lyricization of poetry itself—the historical transformation of many varied poetic genres into the single abstraction of the post-Romantic lyric—is responsible for our current, spectral ideal of a genre powerful enough to overcome our habits of not reading it. But my way of phrasing that idea betrays the problem. The notion that poetry is or ever was one genre is the primary symptom of the lyricization of poetry: the songs, riddles, epigrams, sonnets, epitaphs, *blasons*, lieder, elegies, marches, dialogues, conceits, ballads, epistles, hymns, odes, eclogues, and monodramas considered lyric in the Western tradition before the early nineteenth century were not lyric in the same sense as the poetry that we think of as lyric. The fact that we think of almost all poetry as lyric is the secondary symptom of lyricization. When the stipulative functions of particular genres are collapsed into one big idea of poems as lyrics, then the only function poems can perform in our culture is to become individual or communal ideals. Such ideals might

bind particular groups or subcultures (in slams, for example, or avant-garde blogs, or poetry cafés, or salons, or university, library, and museum reading series), but the more ideally lyric poems and poetry culture have become, the fewer actual poetic genres address readers in specific ways. That ratio is responsible for our twenty-first-century sense that poetry is all-important and at the same time already in its afterlife. (183)

In an effort to avoid the negative consequences of the lyricization of poetry, I chose to explore a variety of poetic genres represented in contemporary American poetry. Because generic expectations significantly affect critical attention to humor, this book explores how aspects of particular poetic genres, such as the prose poem or the epic, facilitate and/or complicate a poem's humor and political commitments. By analyzing a number of poetic genres, this book shows how poetry in its varied and hybrid contemporary genres invites and sustains humor in relation to political engagement.

Beyond avoiding the homogenizing trend of lyricization, this book focuses on humorous poets who are engaged with poetic genres since the friction between humor and poetic genre can produce sharp political critique. I contend that the restrictions and traditions of various poetic genres recall the societal constructs that the poets ridicule. The poets' humorous treatment of their particular poetic genres works to destabilize assumptions about those social structures while simultaneously expanding the reader's understanding of the genres.

A set of conventions or constraints accompanies a text written in a particular literary genre, which will inevitably create certain expectations about a text for a reader. Although these constraints may seem to restrict authorial innovation and even yield passive reading practices, since, to a degree, the reader knows what to expect, humorous engagement with generic conventions can flout these expectations and engage the reader's attention and participation. I argue that humor works with poetic genre to critique dominant cultural narratives and to expose and question the ideologies that create and sustain those narratives. Poetic genre conventions recall the limitations of these cultural narratives and the societal structures that reinforce them. By humorously calling attention to or troubling generic constraints, the poets question the social constructs that the constraints evoke and encourage the reader to think about the possibilities of the poetic genre. This process of destabilization and expansion enacts the thought process necessary to assemble an alternative vision and opens up a space in which to imagine new, less restrictive social constructs.

A significant body of critical work concerning contemporary American political poetry does exist, most of it devoted to poetry that is solemn in nature, not humorous. For example, Carolyn Forche's chapter on the poetry of witness in *The Writer in Politics* (1996) describes poetry that reclaims the "social" from the political, creating poetry of resistance with a space for the personal. Cary Nelson's *Our Last First Poets* (1981), a work that explores the conflict between American poetry after 1960 and American history, focuses on poets who write political, earnest poems, such as Adrienne Rich, Theodore Roethke, and Galway Kinnell. The book includes a chapter on W. S. Merwin, whose work is often humorous, but Merwin's humor is not discussed at any length or shown to relate to the poetry's political concerns in an integral way. Another important work devoted to sober political poetry is Michael Bibby's *Hearts and Minds: Bodies, Poetry, and Resistance in the Vietnam Era* (1996), which explores the role of the body in activist poetry of the Vietnam era, especially Black Liberation, Women's Liberation, and GI Resistance poetry. The poems Bibby examines are often sober, and humor is not one of the work's interests. Other major studies have been produced on feminist poetry and poetry of the Black Arts movement, but, again, these works tend to focus on sober political poetry or to avoid discussion of humor's relation to political critique. A groundbreaking work quoted earlier in this introduction, Philip Metres's *Behind the Lines: War Resistance Poetry on the American Homefront since 1941* (2007), analyzes war resistance poetry from World War II through September 11, 2001, but again, the subject of humor is not broached. This book examines humorous political poetry that has been largely neglected because of its lack of apparent seriousness as well as humorous political poetry which has been treated but in which the humor has not been given its due. By doing so, it shows that humorous political poetry provides qualitatively different opportunities for changing readers' perspectives than its earnest counterpart by demanding active engagement with the text, highlighting the illogic of cultural narratives, and encouraging paradigm shifts.

This project primarily examines the function of humor in the work of four poets writing between the 1960s and 2001—Harryette Mullen, Russell Edson, Edward Dorn, and Marilyn Hacker—chosen because their uses of humor to communicate political critique involve different poetic genres. Though other poets, such as Denise Duhamel and Bob Perelman, feature humorous critiques in their work, their less direct engagement with received genres excludes them from this project since political critique generated by the interplay of humor and poetic genre is its central focus. Edson writes prose poems that complicate narrative expectations. Dorn's long poem *Gunslinger* (1975) draws upon comic books, Western films, traditional epic poetry, and philosophy for its structure.[4] Hacker writes in traditional metrical forms, and Mullen, the most radical experimentalist among them, draws upon Oulipian techniques, such as S+7, in *Sleeping with the Dictionary* (2002). In addition to fostering a richer understanding of their work, focusing on these four poets allows us to explore how varied poetic genres, representative of contemporary American poetry, affect or contribute to political critique and humor. Yet, to show that the intersection of humor, poetic genre, and political critique is not limited to these four poets, each chapter includes discussion of other poets who engage with these attributes in similar ways.

Hacker is paired with R. S. Gwynn, Mullen's work is compared to Terrance Hayes's and Charles Bernstein's, Dorn is discussed in relation to Derek Walcott, and Edson's prose poems are linked to Anne Carson's poetic prose. Of course, these nine poets do not make an exhaustive list of all American poets writing between the 1960s and 2001 who use humor and poetic genre to generate political critique. It is my hope that others will join the critical conversation to expand the scholarship on humor, politics, and genre in contemporary American poetry.

Methodology and Structure

This book contains four chapters, each focused primarily on one of the four poets mentioned above, followed by a brief conclusion. Each chapter focuses on the use of humor in the poetry. The discussion is grounded in close readings and guided by the following questions: How does the poetry employ humor? How does the humor facilitate critiques of specific societal structures or political ideologies or positions and the language that supports them? How does the poetry's manipulation of generic conventions contribute to the humor and the critique? My readings use existing literary criticism devoted to the relationship between poetry and politics. Since little work concerning humor in contemporary American poetry exists, this project draws upon humor theory from varied disciplines.

Almost all humor theorists agree that incongruity is an integral part of humor, which lends itself perfectly to the purposes of social critique. However, as Trousdale asserts about modern poetry, no one humor theory adequately explains the myriad examples of humor in contemporary American poetry (12). For this study I found it necessary to consult and incorporate specific humor theories into my analysis in order to better articulate the structure and function of humor in the different texts. Although

I draw upon classic humor theorists and theories, such as Bergson and Freud, I have attempted to use more recent work in the field of humor theory to develop my arguments. The field itself is varied and includes approaches from numerous disciplines, including sociology, psychology, biology, linguistics, and literary studies. I have selected theories and theorists that help illuminate the specific function and effects of the humor in each poet's work, using the nature of the poet's work, particularly the genre and the subject matter, to determine which theories to apply. Incongruity theory and recent literary theory on wit lend themselves well to Marilyn Hacker's gender-bending sonnet sequence;[5] for Mullen's experimental, procedural poems, linguistic humor theory and sociological humor theory focused on the relationship between race and humor prove useful; sociological humor theories of rebellion, as well as incongruity theory, help to explicate Dorn's mock-epic; and, finally, analysis of Edson's humorous prose poems is enhanced by the application of theories of the absurd and aspects of Bergson's classic theories.

The chapters are organized by poetic genre, beginning with the genres with the most restrictive structures and constraints and moving to more open forms. Hacker writes in traditional, received forms, such as the sonnet, which feature metrical patterns and rhyme schemes. Mullen's procedural poetry builds upon Oulipian traditions and employs a variety of creative constraints. Dorn's expansive, ranging *Gunslinger* draws upon the traditions of the poetic epic. Finally, Edson's prose poetry blurs the boundary between genres. This approach enables me to demonstrate the generic variety of humorous political poetry in the final decades of the twentieth century. As a result, I show different ways particular poets negotiate relationships among poetic genre, humor, and politics; in the conclusion, I observe important commonalities among these varieties of humorous political poetry.

The revived interest in traditional forms in the last few decades has encouraged considerable debate about the politics of poetic forms. Many feminist poets such as Adrienne Rich resisted received forms, arguing that they represent a repressive, patriarchal tradition, which has excluded and degraded women. In contrast, as we see in chapter 1, Marilyn Hacker writes almost exclusively in received forms, with some modern twists. Hacker's decision to write in these forms asserts women's place in the tradition, demonstrating that claiming one's rightful place is an effective form of resistance.

Marilyn Hacker's sonnet sequence, *Love, Death, and the Changing of the Seasons* (1986) tracks the course of a lesbian love affair, often in explicit detail that leaves little to the imagination. Hacker cleverly engages with the history and conventions of the sonnet sequence by expressly calling attention to them and then humorously manipulating them in order to indicate and critique the patriarchal tradition of the genre. Instead of seeming discouraged or limited by the history of the genre, Hacker exuberantly plays with the perceived barriers, encouraging a fresh, expanded understanding of the genre. Contributing to this critique of patriarchy is Hacker's depiction of the lovers' hedonistic lifestyle. By emphasizing the pleasures, both physical and intellectual, that the lovers experience with one another, she shows that this relationship embodies "the good." Her hedonistic value system flouts the dominant heteronormative social values that marginalize homosexuals and deem their sexual orientation as morally objectionable. Her hedonism, which extends and references the literary history of writers using hedonism to articulate political critique, empowers individuals to decide what constitutes "the good," advocating for individual agency and denouncing a moralistic, socially prescribed value system that offers one version of "the good," applicable to all.

Through comparative analysis of R. S. Gwynn's *The Drive In*—Gwynn is considered a key figure in the "New Formalist" movement, a return to writing in received forms marked by political conservatism—I articulate key differences in how the poets use humor to express their political agendas. This comparison highlights how Hacker's poems in *Love, Death, and the Changing of the Seasons* do not simply defend the position of those on the margins of society; they celebrate the possibilities that margins provide, exhibiting a sense of liberation from constricting social norms, making those who uphold those norms seem out of touch and laughable since they are missing out on the good life.

In chapter 2 we see how, unlike Hacker's humor, which is largely generated from the tension between genre conventions of received forms and comical narratives based in the particulars of autobiography, Harryette Mullen's humor often stems from nonnarrative word play, in which the words themselves are the source and focus of the humor. In *Sleeping with the Dictionary*, Mullen's readers are presented with acrostics, abecedarians, and anagrams, among other word games. Using the principles of procedural poetics developed by the Oulipo, Mullen creates poem puzzles that revel in the pleasures of language. Mullen modifies the strict procedural techniques of Oulipo, which often result in largely apolitical texts, to produce more politically engaged poems. In these poems she stresses that capitalism encourages reification, which leads to conceptions of things, ideas, and even other people as static objects. This thought process can result in dehumanization; moreover, as Mullen shows, reification helps to sustain racist and sexist views by facilitating the view of people as objects to be used. Despite the seemingly limiting, predetermined structure of her poems, they positively explode with meanings and possibilities, demonstrating that socially prescribed roles can be exceeded or changed through creativity. Linking Mullen's proceduralism to Terrance Hayes's in a discussion of their anagrammatic play shows the pervasiveness and potential of poets using witty, playful strategies to interrogate identity construction. Through comparisons with another of her contemporaries, Charles Bernstein, who employs similar procedural poetic techniques, I show how Mullen's unique proceduralism is especially well suited to societal critique.

Ed Dorn's long poem *Gunslinger* (1975) incorporates and plays with conventions of the epic, the Western, and the traditional lyric, among other genres. The loosely structured plot follows a motley crew consisting of a whorehouse madam, a pot-smoking, philosophizing horse, and a demigod gunslinger, on their quest to find and confront the elusive Robart, a character based on Howard Hughes. The heterogeneity of the text emphasizes how American capitalism appropriates and blends dominant cultural narratives, such as the American dream and Christianity, in order to thrive. The protean Howard Hughes figure has many aliases and disguises that recall, conflate, and confuse these narratives, making their manipulation by the powers that be apparent and thus easier for individuals to interrogate and critique. By challenging the reader to make sense of the tangled cultural narratives, Dorn replicates the thought process of a critically engaged citizen. Active participation in one's society is shown to be an important step to counter the development of the military-industrial complex. Contrasting Dorn's work with another work that humorously engages with the epic genre, I use Derek Walcott's *Omeros*, which demonstrates the great potential for humorous political critique that the epic provides.

Russell Edson's prose poems, which are the subject of chapter 4, blur genre boundaries. They read like mutated narratives and fables, encourage readers to re-view the world, and question the status quo through their dark, uncomfortable humor, often generated by violating the reader's narrative expectations. Edson's poems, unlike traditional fables, do not present easily translatable scenarios in order to provide the reader with a tidy moral lesson. They question the logic of such narratives through absurd imagery and situations, making ideas or practices that seem customary emerge as strange or arbitrary. Humanist ideals, which encourage egocentrism and speciesism, are the frequent target of Edson's critique. In his poems, humans, animals, and inanimate objects possess similar capabilities, such as the ability to speak and reason. By highlighting the similarities of these individuals, Edson humorously emphasizes the ridiculousness and prevalence of human egocentrism and anthropocentrism. In his posthuman world the human characters stubbornly cling to humanist values, which frequently results in conflict, making the world a dangerous, violent one. This violence is at the heart of Edson's critique. Clinging to speciesism in order to bolster the fragile human ego results in damage to nonhumans and humans alike. A brief comparative analysis of Anne Carson's *Autobiography of Red* suggests that prose poetry as a genre has great potential for questioning the limits of narrative.

As the conclusion of this study will make clear, although political poetry is often seen as aggressive or angry because of its critical agenda, and humor is often discussed as a release of aggression or in terms of its disciplinary capabilities, these poets produce work that is ultimately uplifting. This is not to say that their work is naïve or devoid of vitriol. To be sure, theirs is no sappy greeting-card verse with trite phrases that fall flat and seem insincere, but underneath the groan-worthy puns, dirty jokes, and scathing satire is the hope that if we laugh at what is wrong with our world and ourselves, we might be reminded of our kinship with others. We might be inspired to try and make some things right.

CHAPTER ONE

The Good Life

The Politics of Hedonism in Marilyn Hacker's
Love, Death, and the Changing of the Seasons

Marilyn Hacker's *Love, Death, and the Changing of the Seasons* is an apt choice to begin an exploration of the interplay among humor, political critique, and poetic genre since the book-length sonnet sequence features, arguably, one of the most famous poetic forms in Western literature, and its humor is raucous and bawdy. Hacker's Dionysian treatment of the subjects of food, drink, shopping, and sex animate the book. Her fantasies include descriptions of sumptuous meals, as we can see in "Lacoste IV" when she describes a "cassoulet / with goose from Carcassonne" (25). The care and specificity with which she recalls one meal with a friend and her daughter in "Grand Hotel Malher" illustrates how she revels in fine cuisine:

> at the Basque local, "Le Fandango."
> Jackie and I had magret de canard,
> and split a Mercurey (rouge) to our hard
> times, while Iva devoured *escargots*. (31)

In the epistolary poem "Dear Julie, here's your regular Sunday," she tells a friend about the new activities that she, her lover Ray, and Hacker's daughter Iva have been trying lately, and food dominates the events on the list, including a lobster dinner and "gorging"

> on a tray
> of seafood antipasto that reminded
> me of those *grandes bouffes* in the Via dei
> Marci. (110)

And, in "Bloomingdale's I," Hacker combines indulgences, which she often does, in a sexual shopping fantasy,[1] the speaker exclaiming to her lover, "'If we saw anything we liked, we'd buy it!'" before describing the sexual acts she would perform on her lover in the changing room, "'You'd pull my hair. You'd have to bite your tongue. / I'd hold your ass so that you wouldn't fall'" (83, quotation marks original).

Hacker's use of these subjects has been recognized by critics, most notably by Mary Biggs in her article "Bread and Brandy: Food and Drink in the Poetry of Marilyn Hacker." Characterizing the general role of food and drink in Hacker's poetry, Biggs writes, "the food is fresh, delicious, perfectly cooked and presented; the drink is ideal in temperature and effect; and both not only symbolize life's joys but seem literally essential to joy: to discovery, sex, love, communication, companionship, nurturance, positive potential, homemaking" (130).

To this list of joys I would add poetic creation, as food and drink frequently surface in Hacker's poems about the process of writing. Biggs, in this article and in her more recent "'Present, Infinitesimal, Infinite': The Political Vision and 'Femin' Poetics of Marilyn Hacker," connects this imagery to Hacker's theme of exile and uses it to describe Hacker's feminism since it may represent home and domesticity.[2] I see broader political significance in this imagery, which I read as joyful in a specifically hedonistic sense as it displays a passionate reveling in the pleasures of life, particularly in Hacker's book-length sonnet sequence about her relationship with a younger woman, *Love, Death, and the Changing of the Seasons*. Hacker's recurring sensual subjects indicate a hedonistic worldview, one that uses pleasure to determine what is good—both in terms of fulfillment and doing what is ethical—instead of relying upon cultural norms to define what makes a life good. Hacker's sonnet sequence demonstrates that a life given over to pleasure, whether gleaned from food, drink, love, sex, art, family, intellectual stimulation, etc., is the good life.

The interplay of Marilyn Hacker's hedonism, use of traditional poetic forms, and humor—a humor which alternatively creates or is produced by hedonistic revelry—helps her to critique dominant/normative (patriarchal, heterosexual) cultural narratives of love with a minimal amount of didacticism. The nondidactic quality of her work sets her poems apart from much of the politically charged poetry written by her contemporaries and helps her to avoid overly prescriptive declarations of what is right or wrong while simultaneously critiquing the limiting moral pronouncements of others. She shows that lesbian romance is part of the tradition of love poetry; it has only been overshadowed by patriarchal, normative representations of love. Emphasizing the hedonistic aspects of her love affair, both sensory and intellectual, is a political act. By incorporating different aspects of hedonism and drawing upon the tradition of hedonistic writers, Hacker offers her work as a model of the good life in hedonistic terms.

Using pleasure as a measure of value creates a system that focuses on situational ethical concerns as opposed to systems that rely upon a predetermined set of morals to determine right from wrong. This focus strips the power away from others to judge whether a person's life is good or bad based upon social norms. Like the Decadent and Aesthetic Movements, Hacker's presentation of hedonistic values disrupts the status quo and places the onus of moral responsibility on the individual instead of on society. Hacker's poems do not simply defend the position of those on the margins of society; they celebrate the possibilities that margins provide, challenging readers to rethink the social values that relegate people to the outskirts. The celebration of a life portrayed throughout the sonnet sequence goes beyond lobbying for acceptance; it exhibits a sense of liberation from constricting social norms, making those who uphold them seem out of touch and laughable since they are missing out on the good life.

Hedonism has a long, often confusing, history, and it has many iterations. At one end of the spectrum is Aristippean hedonism, which is more Dionysian in nature in that it values sensory pleasures over mental ones and immediate pleasures over potential long-term ones (Feldman 30–32). At the more conservative end is Epicureanism, which values mental and long-term pleasures as well as friendship and "a life of tranquil reflection" (Feldman 91). Although the basic philosophical principle of hedonism involves accepting pleasure as the only good, there are common misperceptions and numerous objections, usually moral in nature, to the concept. A classic misunderstanding of hedonist philosophy is that hedonism is all about sensory pleasures. On the contrary, mental and intellectual pleasures figure prominently in hedonistic philosophy and in Hacker's written performance of a hedonistic life. Another misapprehension of hedonism is that the object that provides pleasure is intrinsically good. A more accurate representation of hedonism is that if someone takes pleasure from listening to a thunderstorm at night, the thunderstorm is not intrinsically good, the person's attitude toward it (one of pleasure) is.

Because of these misunderstandings, it is useful to look at a specific, quite inclusive, definition of hedonism before proceeding with textual analysis. Fred Feldman, a contemporary philosopher and self-proclaimed hedonist, has formulated the concept of

Intrinsic Attitudinal Hedonism, which falls near the middle of the spectrum of hedonism. His definition of hedonism accurately describes the hedonism portrayed in Hacker's sonnet sequence: "the fundamental bearers of intrinsic value are episodes in which someone takes intrinsic *attitudinal* pleasure or pain in something, rather than in episodes in which someone feels *sensory* pleasure or pain" (Feldman 66; italics in original). Feldman's concept does not discount sensory pleasure; indeed he claims that many sensory pleasures lead to attitudinal pleasures, but he does not restrict pleasures to the sensory realm. His concept blends aspects of various definitions of hedonism, including the conservative Epicureanism and the Dionysian, sensory-based hedonism of Aristippus. This concept seems in line with Hacker's hedonism in *Love, Death, and the Changing of the Seasons* because she just as often describes mental pleasures, such as reading, writing and conversing, as she does sensory ones. More importantly, attitudinal hedonism, because of its focus on an individual's perception, allows each individual to decide what is pleasurable, and, by extension, what is good.

Feldman delineates three key tenets of Intrinsic Attitudinal Hedonism:

 i. *Every episode of intrinsic attitudinal pleasure is intrinsically good; every episode of intrinsic attitudinal pain is intrinsically bad.*
 ii. *The intrinsic value of an episode of intrinsic attitudinal pleasure is equal to the amount of pleasure contained in that episode; the intrinsic value of an episode of intrinsic attitudinal pain is equal to—(the amount of pain contained in that episode).*
 iii. *The intrinsic value of a life is entirely determined by the intrinsic values of the episodes of intrinsic attitudinal pleasure and pain contained in this life, in such a way that one life is intrinsically better than another if and only if the net amount of intrinsic attitudinal pleasure in the one is greater than the net amount of that sort of pleasure in the other.* (66; italics in original)

In this formulation, since the value of a life is determined by the amount of pleasure and pain—as perceived and experienced by each individual—it is up to each individual to decide if their life has been a good one or not. This internal determination of what constitutes a good life does not rely upon fixed, socially prescribed moral codes. It consequently frees people whose lives do not fit those external standards to possess their own value system. Such a value system allows marginalized people, such as Hacker and other members of the LGBTQI[3] community, to assess themselves on their terms. As Feldman maintains, in attitudinal hedonism "there are no worthless pleasures, or defeated pleasures, or transvalued pleasures" (66; italics in original). Importantly, Feldman's theory does not judge specific sources of pleasure as good or bad, only a person's attitudinal response to them.

> Look what we're making, besides love (that has a name to speak). (106)

The allusion to "the love that dare not speak its name" in the above lines from Hacker's "Having Kittens About Having Babies III" points to the literary precedents of her hedonistic, nondidactic, yet politically charged poetry. The phrase, which played an important role in Oscar Wilde's indecency trial, is drawn from a poem by Lord Alfred Douglas, Oscar Wilde's younger lover. Indeed, Hacker alludes to numerous other writers with hedonistic leanings, which shows her awareness of hedonism's literary lineage. Oscar Wilde is a principal figure in the history of hedonism in literature, and an examination of his hedonistic philosophies can enhance our understanding of the political role hedonism plays in Hacker's work:

> I can resist everything except temptation.
> Pleasure is the only thing to live for. Nothing ages like happiness.

A cigarette is the perfect type of pleasure; it is exquisite and leaves one unsatisfied.
One can never pay too high a price for any sensation. (Wilde, *Epigrams*, 11, 20, 38, 41)

This small sampling of Wilde's epigrams along with the "new hedonism" described in *The Picture of Dorian Gray* are just a few examples of hedonistic thought in his oeuvre. The above bons mots are amusing, but they also point to Wilde's aesthetic and political philosophies. As in Hacker's writing, humor is integral to Wilde's nondidactic political critique.

Wilde is associated with the Aesthetic and Decadent Movements. The two movements, due in part to their rejection of Victorian morality, are closely related and often equated with one another, but there are a few important distinctions between them. Michael Patrick Gillespie states that writers of the Aesthetic Movement "subscribed to the doctrine that art represents the supreme value because it stands as self-sufficient and has no aim beyond its own perfection. To this end, they asserted that the function of a work of art lies simply in its existence and in its ability to exude beauty, indifferent to current social values" (142). Although the Aesthetic Movement may seem apolitical or amoral because of its emphasis on pleasure, focusing on pleasure created an opportunity to envision a different system of morality, while focusing on artistic freedom asserted the right to express views that differed from societal norms. As Wilde would write in *The Picture of Dorian Gray*, "Modern morality consists in accepting the standard of one's age" (63).

The Decadent Movement was more extreme in its views: "With a self-conscious and restless curiosity, the Decadents placed art as supreme to Nature, and they attacked accepted standards through over-refined sensibilities and aggressive perversion of convention" (Gillespie 142). Similar to Hacker's middle-ground hedonism, Wilde's sensibilities seem to lie somewhere in the middle,[4] but whether one considers Wilde a Decadent or an Aesthete, his relentless questioning of convention, like Hacker's, is undeniable.

J. Edward Chamberlain's explanation of decadence in his book on Wilde and his contemporaries hinges on the idea of subordination: "The style which is called decadent, therefore, is primarily distinguished by its subordination of the whole for the benefit of its parts, and in this respect is distinct from a classical style in which the parts of the whole are secondary to the harmonies achieved by the entire structure" (Chamberlain 95). Although this definition undoubtedly encapsulates the movement's focus on aesthetics and pleasure, the sociopolitical implications are more interesting. Subordination, with its implications of subservience and inferiority, recalls social hierarchies. Instead of accepting the conventional attitudes ("the whole"), Wilde and other Decadents wish to give a voice to different and differing parts that may have been silenced or drowned out by the whole, an illustration of what Dellamora identifies as the radical quality of decadence: its "opposition to the organization of modern urban, industrial, and commercial society" (529). Decadence, then, points to a shift from a collective view of society and social norms to an individualistic one in which a focus on the parts exceeds the confines of the whole.

It seems no coincidence that Wilde is famous for his epigrams, for the epigram as a literary utterance performs the subordination of the whole to the parts. Bruce Michelson eloquently writes in *Literary Wit* of epigrams in a literary context (which many of Wilde's most famous originally were): "For at least an instant, a literary epigram can shame an entire apparatus of thought, complicate or disrupt some unexamined system. . . . It can tug at the threads of an ideological fabric normally taken for granted, and open a possibility that all can come undone" (34). Epigrams are "disruptive" in the sense that they encourage readers to consider accepted ideas in a new light. They make the parts more conspicuous than the whole as plays on individual words (the parts) become the focus, interrupting and disrupting the thought process. This interruption provides opportunity for reflection, allowing readers to see how those parts and what they stand for might be differently arranged, thereby potentially revising paradigms.

The compression of the epigram enhances these moments of disruption, as we can see in Wilde's famous example, "I can resist everything except temptation" (*Epigrams* 11). The first four words boast about the speaker's self-control. The reader expects the exception to be a minor indulgence, like chocolate or wine, since people rarely brag about giving into their desires (one assumes ceding to desires certainly would not have been common cause for boasting during Wilde's era of Victorian conservatism). The final word surprises, amuses, and disrupts, while making an uncanny kind of sense: of course people can resist something if it does not tempt them. Although this epigram expresses Wilde's hedonism, it also pokes fun at the unnaturalness of his society, which suppresses human desires in order to adhere to artificial, arbitrary standards of morality. This type of directed, disruptive joking, as Peter Michelson states, "affirms the intellectual liberty of the reader" and encourages them to rethink accepted norms (34).

Although Marilyn Hacker and Oscar Wilde specialized in different genres and focused on dissimilar subject matters, Hacker's work is disruptive in the way that Wilde's is.[5] Her sharp wit, humor, and hedonism play important and surprising political roles in her work. Like the compression of Wilde's epigrams, the tight formal restraints of Hacker's poems, especially when coupled with humor, create instances of explosive subversion. Indeed, the sonnet, especially the Shakespearean sonnet, is often described as epigrammatic because the closing couplet lends itself to pithy witticisms. In *Love, Death, and the Changing of the Seasons*, Hacker uses the sonnet form to emphasize her marginalized status as a lesbian, a part silenced by the whole, and critiques the status quo in true hedonistic fashion. In the poem "Having Kittens About Having Babies II," for instance, Hacker addresses the socially prescribed differences between heterosexual and homosexual couples,[6] extending a theme from lines in the previous poem: "because /

no law defines this love, we are outlaws. / We're not, each to the other, marginal" (105). Although the lesbian lovers are "not, each to the other, marginal," Hacker describes their subordinate status in the heteronormative culture in the next poem in the sequence, "Having Kittens About Having Babies III." She begins the poem describing heteronormative couples: "They get to make their loves the focal point / of Real Life: last names, trust funds, architecture, / reify them" (106). The heteronormative "they" do not just get to share love without consequences, they get to publicly declare it and slap it on buildings in "Real Life," the capitalization of which makes the lives of the lower-case "we" describing the lesbian couple seem less legitimate: "while we are, they conjecture, / erotic *frissons*, birds of passage, quaint /embellishments in margins" (106). The characterization of "we" as fleeting ("erotic *frissons*" and "birds of passage") and superfluous "quaint embellishments in margins" relegates them to the outskirts and disparages their loves and lives. By the time the speaker writes "Self-restraint / is failing me, and you, dear heart, suspect your / old trout's about to launch into a lecture," the reader is probably harboring similar suspicions (106). However, even though it would be justified, the speaker cheekily replies, "I ain't," and does not launch into a diatribe about unequal civil rights. Instead, she responds with a hedonistic gesture by repeatedly demanding "serious long" kisses from her lover, performing indulgence. Replacing a lecture with acts of pleasure rebuffs the limited and limiting worldview held by "they." What better way to discount those views than by reveling in what they deem insignificant?

By humorously rhyming "Self-restraint," a term that, on one level, recalls the "restraint" the sonnet form requires, with "I ain't," a slang term not usually associated with the formality of the sonnet, Hacker calls attention to and playfully mocks the poem's form and mimics the poem's critique of societal constraints. This humor, like Wilde's, prevents Hacker's critique from lapsing into didacticism, but it does not make it less politically efficacious. In Biggs's article

"'Present, Infinitesimal, Infinite': The Political Vision and 'Femin' Poetics of Marilyn Hacker," she coins the term "femin" to describe Hacker's feminism, claiming that it goes against traditional notions of feminism because it is not didactic and it foregrounds domestic pursuits. Biggs claims that after Hacker's second collection her poems

> are not fired by apparent didactic "purpose," a word which is key to my definition of feminist poetry: purpose to exonerate or extol womanhood, or to develop gendered consciousness or expand its scope from the individual to the collective, or to rouse to action. Poetry attempting to fulfill this kind of purpose can be effective; I argue only that Marilyn Hacker's poetry does not and, thus, demands a new name. (6)

I disagree with this interpretation of Hacker's feminism. Just because Hacker's poetry is not didactic in its representations of feminism does not mean that it is any less feminist or merits its own category. It seems to me that a poem that is not fueled by apparent didactic purpose should not be assumed necessarily to lack such a purpose. How does the lack of apparent didacticism make a poem or poet less feminist?

Besides illustrating Hacker's nondidactic feminism, "Having Kittens About Having Babies III" alludes to a famous literary depiction of homosexuality, as was mentioned at the beginning of this section. The humorous "I ain't" is followed up by a pun on a phrase long used to describe homosexual relationships: "Look what we're mak- / ing, besides love (that has a name to speak)." It is worth noting that in his indecency trial defense Wilde defined "the love that dare not speak its name" as being between an older man and a younger one. Because Hacker's romance depicts the love—and the challenges that such love presents—between an older and younger woman, seen most obviously in this poem by Hacker's self-referential "old trout," this allusion is particularly apt. When Wilde was asked to explain the phrase in his trial he responded:

It is beautiful, it is fine, it is the noblest form of affection. There is nothing unnatural about it. It is intellectual, and it repeatedly exists between an elder and a younger man, when the elder man has intellect, and the younger man has all the joy, hope and glamour of life before him. That it should be so, the world does not understand. The world mocks at it and sometimes puts one in the pillory for it. (Linder)

In her poem, Hacker flouts the idea that homosexual love need be unspoken or unnamed, and she also indicates that, through their meeting of minds and artistic creation, they are making something more pleasurable, and, therefore better in hedonistic terms, than the reified trust funds and buildings of heteronormative love. Wilde stated in his indecency trial that "the love that dare not speak its name" is "intellectual, and it repeatedly exists between an elder and younger man, when the elder has the intellect, and the younger man has all the joy, hope and glamour of life before him." Hacker's relationship with Ray holds many of those characteristics. Hacker is the poetry teacher and Ray is a brilliant and burgeoning poet. They have sonnet races to see who can produce one of merit in the shortest time. Ray is just beginning, in Hacker's words, her "brilliant career" (129), as we can see in "We suit you up to go and knock them dead," a sonnet depicting Ray and Hacker at a poetry conference—where Hacker seems to know most of the attendees—during which they prepare Ray for a big event, presumably an interview or a reading (130).

The intellectual, artistic product of Hacker and Ray's relationship is of great value. The final quatrain of "Having Kittens About Having Babies III," implies that the love between the speaker and Ray will be immortalized in poetry, something with "openness" that will live on through its readers and their interpretations (106). As Lynn Keller points out, "the relationship these lesbian feminists are creating is expansive (open), and the work it is doing is substantial. No doubt Hacker holds similar aspirations for the sonnet sequences they are making" (284). Beyond the previously mentioned implication of the immortality of poetry, the "openness" of their creation performs a lesbian life and love lived in the open. Although their creation is art for the sake of art, it is also art, like Wilde's, that is "radical in its opposition to the organization of modern, urban, industrial, and commercial society" (Dellamora 529). It challenges the limiting, heteronormative, socially accepted expressions of romantic love.

Another of Wilde's famous epigrams, "Life imitates art far more than art imitates Life," helps to illustrate the nature of the poem's subversiveness (*Epigrams* 53). The text is a representation of what life should imitate, of how life should be: it should celebrate all kinds of lives and loves instead of forcing some to the margins. In the poem's last line, the speaker designated William Blake, known for his liberal, hedonistic views on sexuality and desire—as well as his penchant for epigrammatic writing, e.g., "The road of excess leads to the palace of wisdom"—as "Cousin." One cannot help but think that Hacker would also claim Wilde as kin.

The intellectual connection between Hacker and Ray enables them to create instances of pleasure in their texts. The concept of the pleasure of the text comes from yet another hedonist writer, Roland Barthes, and helps to illuminate the important role that formalism plays in Hacker's political critique. In *The Pleasure of the Text* Barthes distinguishes between texts of pleasure and texts of bliss:

> Text of pleasure: the text that contents, fills, grants euphoria; the text that comes from culture and does not break with it, is linked to a *comfortable* practice of reading. Text of bliss: the text that imposes a state of loss, the text that discomforts (perhaps to the point of a certain boredom), unsettles the reader's historical, cul-

tural, psychological assumptions, the consistency of his tastes, values, memories, brings to a crisis his relation with language. (14)

The translation of Barthes's terminology from French to English has caused some confusion. "Pleasure" and "bliss," though "bliss" conveys a more intense state than does "pleasure," are less distinct in English, but *plaisir* and *jouissance*, Barthes's terms, have distinct meanings, which Robert Miklitsch has translated as "forepleasure" and "orgasm" respectively. Texts of pleasure, then, are "comfortable" or less intense, while texts of bliss are disruptive.

As several critics have indicated, although the above description seems to draw clear differences between the text of pleasure and the text of bliss, they are not mutually exclusive categories. Robert Miklitsch posits that Barthes "problematizes the undecidable difference of the pleasure of the text by internalizing the texts ("pleasure"/"bliss") within the reading/writing subject, one who simultaneously reads as he writes, and vice versa" (105). He claims that "a particular text is neither wholly a "text of pleasure" nor a "text of bliss": it is *always already* both" (105). This both/and explanation of texts of pleasure and texts of bliss suggests a constant tension between the two categories. Indeed, it seems that a text of bliss could not generate moments of disruption without possessing elements of pleasure.

In the introduction to *The Pleasure of the Feminist Text*, it is precisely this "undecidable difference" that Susanne Gruss uses to explain her title's play on Barthes's *The Pleasure of the Text*. Gruss claims, and I agree, that such "positive ambiguity" is an attribute common to much feminist writing (7).[7] *Love, Death, and the Changing of the Seasons* provides a *"comfortable* practice of reading" insofar as its use of traditional forms participates in high cultural history (Barthes 14). Yet, it is precisely the context of the traditional, "comfortable" poetic genre of the sonnet sequence that enables its portrayal of a lesbian love story told through direct, and often crude language, including graphic descriptions of sex, to "[unsettle] the reader's historical, cultural, psychological assumptions, the consistency of his" or her or their "tastes, values, memories, brings to a crisis his relation with language" (Barthes 14). The tension between the genre and the content yields many instances of humorous incongruity, or of bliss. These humorous disruptions help Hacker to espouse cultural critique without being overly moralistic and to enhance the pleasure of the text.

Elliott Oring's "appropriate incongruity" theory of humor helps to explain how these moments of humorous disruption function in the text. He claims that humor "depends upon the perception of an *appropriate incongruity*; that is, the perception of an appropriate relationship between categories that would ordinarily be regarded as incongruous" (1). Oring explains his theory by contrasting it with the more familiar incongruity-resolution theory of humor: "the term *appropriate incongruity* does not suggest that an incongruity is *resolved*" (2; italics original). This theory of humor aptly describes the way humor functions in Hacker's work. There is not a resolution between the incongruous elements, which are often genre expectations clashing with blunt, modern language. Rather, the reader recognizes the incongruity, but does not have the comfortable satisfaction of resolving it. The remaining unsettling excess creates moments of disruptive bliss.

In her short piece "Meditating Formally," written for the volume *A Formal Feeling Comes: Poems in Form by Contemporary Women*, Marilyn Hacker writes of the pleasures of composing and reading poetry in fixed forms. Although traditional verse would seem to fall under the rubric of "texts of pleasure," the orgasmic bodily sensations she describes to illustrate the feelings associated with reading and writing poetry in fixed forms seem in line with Barthes's designation of a "text of bliss":

> The choice and use of a fixed or structured form—whether I learned it or invented it—has always been, for me, one of the primary pleasures of writing poetry. I have no political or aesthetic

rationale for it, except that I like it. The intersection of that very sensory/sensual satisfaction, related to music, related to walking, breathing, all the rhythmic bodily motions, and the emotional or intellectual difficulty, complexity, of the narrative, lyric or meditative treatment of certain subjects creates a tension that is, for me, a mental equivalent of those physical states where pleasure approaches pain, or pain, pleasure—whether the activity involved is sex or hiking. (*New Expansive Poetry* 177)

Characterizing verse in fixed forms as "a mental equivalent of those physical states where pleasure approaches pain, or pain, pleasure" links it to a text of bliss that "discomforts." Poetry in traditional forms may seem far from radical verse that destabilizes readers' and writers' relationship to language, but Hacker's description of the "heightened awareness" of language that such forms demand troubles that assumption. Indeed, Hacker's choice of form enables moments of bliss (*New Expansive Poetry* 177).

Although in the above quotation Hacker claims her choice to write in fixed or received forms is not politically motivated, elsewhere she affirms that her choice to write in received forms is a hedonistic act and consequently a political performance. In an interview with Karla Hammond, Hacker reveals her recognition of the political implications of the choice to write in traditional forms:

Traditional forms or, for that matter, invented forms aren't in any way inimical to women's poetry, or contemporary poetry. It is important for women writers to reclaim the tradition, to rediscover and redefine our place in it and lay claim to our considerable contributions, innovations, and inventions. Traditional narrative and lyric forms have been used by women for centuries—even if our professors of Western literature never mentioned Marie de France or Christine de Pisan. The language that we use was as much created and invented by women as by men. But generation after generation, women's contributions get edged out, written out. (22)

As Keller indicates, Hacker's stance is counter to that of Adrienne Rich who at midcareer viewed writing in received forms "as emotionally or politically repressive, as incapable of capturing authentic or individual speech" (261). Hacker claims that our language is not "the master's language," but that women's parts in its creation have been drowned out by the patriarchy.

This stance not only differentiates Hacker from Rich but also from the group of poets often referred to as the New Formalists. Hacker has been anthologized within that group, which Mark Jarman and David Mason define in the preface to their book *Rebel Angels: 25 Poets of the New Formalism* as American poets writing formalist poetry born after the 1940s (xix). Jarmin and Mason characterize the movement as a revolution—indeed, "revolution" is the first word of the preface (xv)—but many other critics note the conservatism of the New Formalists. Ira Sadoff in his article "Neo-formalism: a Dangerous Nostalgia" deems the movement politically conservative, dominated by white men, longing for a simpler past. He describes the poets' "desire for universality, an ideology which disguises its refusal to acknowledge difference" connecting it to their "high regard for impersonality and tonal distance" (9). As we have seen, Hacker's work celebrates difference and foregrounds the personal, creating a progressive political vision. Perhaps comparison is the best way to see the difference that Sadoff describes between Hacker's poetry and that produced by the New Formalists.

In *Rebel Angels* Hacker's work appears directly after R. S. Gwynn's. Most of Gwynn's selections come from his 1986 book *The Drive In*, published the same year as *Love, Death, and the Changing of the Seasons*. Gwynn's first poem in *Rebel Angels*, "Among Philistines," which is also the opening poem in *The Drive In*, is a modern retelling of the story of Samson and Delilah. In Gwynn's version, Samson's role in his fate is downplayed and Delilah is both hypersexualized and demonized. She's recast as an actress who stars in films in the nude. An ad promoting Delilah's film about her betrayal of Samson depicts her "naked, sucking on a pair / Of golden shears, winking her lewdest smile / Amid a monumental pile of hair." Samson notes "how his locks demurely hid / Her tits and snatch. And how her lips were red" (Gwynn 10). Although Hacker also uses crude language in her poems and frequently writes about sex, her work focuses on mutual sexual relationships, and does not include objectifying, flat descriptions of women like Gwynn's Delilah.

Later in Gwynn's poem Samson pleads with God to "Return that strength of which I have been shorn, / That we might smite this tasteless *shiksa* land" (10). The poem both objectifies Delilah and deems the entire culture as a "tasteless" feminine one deserving of violent revolt. The fact that Gwynn casts this commercialized, lowbrow culture as feminine is an aggressive stance that runs counter to the politics of Hacker's poetry. The feminine culture that Hacker describes is one of refined taste and and of pleasures: physical, emotional, and intellectual. The title of Gwynn's poem, while an obvious reference to the Philistines in the Samson and Delilah story, can be read as Gwynn's critique of his own culture, of feeling like he lives among those who do not appreciate or understand the arts, maybe his art of writing poetry in received forms in particular. Gwynn and Samson's response to this unfavorable environment differs markedly from Hacker's response to her own unwelcoming society. The ending of "Among Philistines" casts Samson's blinding as "a blessing in disguise," as if being blinded were the only way to endure a culture that seems hostile (10). Hacker's response to a culture that does not accept or celebrate her way of loving and living is to create her own world of pleasure and luxuriate in it, a much less violent, more productive approach.

Returning to Hacker's textual pleasures, lines from "Sweetheart, all day I've been listless and lame," a sonnet describing a poetry class session that Hacker taught, further illustrate the *jouissance* of "meditating formally." As the title implies, the speaker lacks energy and feels low, after being high on intellectual stimulation in class the night before:

> Class night: osmotic energy
> got all the girls in gear. Tight forms to tame
> only made them write funkier, slang
> their diction down. (86)

That the "Tight forms" made the students "slang / their diction down" is a phenomenon Hacker discussed in an interview with Hammond: "I like the tension in a poem that comes from the diction of ordinary speech playing against a form. When there is an internal or external form to be worked with and worked against, unexpected and illuminating things can happen in the piece of writing. This is always fascinating" (22). These moments of tension act like moments of bliss in that they "fascinate" and arrest the reader/writer, disrupting their comfortable reading experience.

It is interesting to note that Hacker chooses to describe the tension between form and ordinary speech as playful. It is this type of play that generates much of the humor in Hacker's work, as we can see in "Which didn't deter me from lying down," a sonnet depicting the speaker masturbating while fantasizing about Ray. This poem, at first, seems as far removed as possible from sonnets found in traditional sonnet sequences, which depict a speaker, usually male, praising or pining for an idealized lover, usually female, from a distance. However, the speaker, though female, is pining for her actual lover from a distance, although at this point in the sequence they have not consummated their relationship; but instead of wallowing in sorrow, she takes matters literally into her own hands. The situation is similar to those depicted in traditional love sonnets, but the candid description of masturbation seems out of place in the form, yielding humorous appropriate incongruity, to use Oring's term, through tension between the form and the language. The language in this poem, moreover, is self-consciously humorous with the self-mocking parenthetical "(what corn)" and the pun-filled lines, "it's Mother Superior on a binge / with laughing gas inflating her bad habit," which play on a nun's typical clothing and masturbation's classification as a bad habit, especially by many religions (36). However, the following line is especially humorous as it seems composed mainly for the sake of fitting in with the poem's rhyme scheme rhyming "rabbit" with "habit": "(If you eat pussy, why won't you eat rabbit?)" (36). It's a parenthetical remark in a poem with several others, but the others serve practical purposes and seem much less random. The first, "(what corn)," is self-mocking, the second, "(I didn't muck up the upholstery, Jax.)," reassures the friend whose couch was the site of self-gratification, and the third, "(Iva took a break from me to read in the hotel room.)," explains how the speaker, who is traveling with her daughter, was able to have this self-indulgent moment in the first place (36). This last one, a question addressed to the absent lover, though sexual in nature, turns from the topic of masturbation and/or overactive libido to culinary preferences for a brief moment, then the poem quickly returns focus to the speaker's thoughts about her relationship. As Keller observes, "Hacker sometimes so pushes the limits of the sonnet that her poems parody the form and the rules determining it" (273). By calling attention to the form through this unexpected, humorous line/rhyme, Hacker blissfully unsettles her reader and his or her expectations of what a love sonnet looks like.

The poem's closing couplet: "It's what in this bright world I would like best: / your mind on my mind; your breasts on my breasts" (36), alludes to a concept with ties to both hedonistic philosophy and homosexual literary history: "the marriage of true minds." The phrase references both Shakespeare's sonnet 116, which depicts "William Shakespeare's idealized friendship with a young man, whom many have identified with William Herbert, first Earl of Pembroke" and "Oscar Wilde's fictional recasting of the debate over the identity of this friend in his short story "The Portrait of Mr. W. H." (Dellamora 531). Additionally, as Richard Dellamora indicates, after her female partner and fellow writer Radclyffe Hall died, Una Troubridge used the phrase to describe their relationship (529–30). Hacker continues the literary tradition of this phrase by alluding to it in "Substitute Teacher," a poem in which the speaker, writing from Europe, describes Ray's experience as a student in her writing workshop with a friend, Marie, at the helm instead of herself. The title literally indicates that Marie is taking on Hacker's teaching duties while the latter is abroad, but it implies the possibility of Marie standing in for Hacker on a personal level as well. Just as Shakespeare was writing to a younger man in Sonnet 116, so too is Ray junior to both Hacker and Marie. The poem is rife with sexual overtones from Marie "staring" Ray "down a bit," to "'Your place or mine?'" which, when coupled with the history of the phrase "marriage of true minds," encourage the following lines to be read as intellectual and sexual fantasy: "I know that every woman in the class / will at least fantasize a *tete a tete* / with her, after, sure that her mind's met / theirs already" (42). The closing lines with their humorous indication of Hacker's jealousy, further illustrate the dual intellectual and sexual meanings of the concept of the marriage of minds: "I hope you two, together in some bar, / talk about us, and poetry, before / my dawn's your midnight, and your door is shut" (42). Although Hacker wishes that Marie and Ray do talk after class, she wants them to talk about "us," meaning Hacker and Ray as a couple, before anything else. Indeed, the phrase ",and poetry," set off by commas, seems like an afterthought on Hacker's part, even though the poem is ostensibly about a poetry workshop. The closing clause "and your door is shut" suggests Hacker's desire for Marie to serve only as a substitute poetry teacher, not as a substitute lover. She wants their minds, and only their minds, to meet, but not to wed.

    The idea of the marriage of true minds is related to certain tenets of Epicurean hedonism. As described by Fred Feldman,

"Epicurus encouraged his students to retire from the world and to live in small communities of like-minded people. The pleasures of communal living with dear friends make for a tranquil and happy life" (102). Living with "like-minded" people and frequently engaging in intellectual discussion and contemplation, in Epicurean terms, is an essential part of the Good Life, in which Hacker and Ray eventually, if temporarily, participate as we can see in the fifth sonnet of the mini sequence "Eight Days in April." The poem begins with Hacker defining her living space as separate from Ray's, "My House" and "yours," but those lines of demarcation quickly begin to blur (69). Hacker is wearing Ray's pajamas and thinking about making duplicate keys so that they can share their three living spaces in New York and Paris. She then muses about what they can teach each other, again recalling the idea of the marriage of true minds. Finally, moving beyond the realm of practical concerns like keys and driving lessons, Hacker describes a more metaphorical, communal space, when she writes, "I think the world's our house" (69). The plural possessive "our" erases boundaries and joins Hacker and Ray in a shared life. The subsequent lines describe an Epicurean realm with Hacker and Ray removed from the world and focused on each other and their intellectual pursuits, "alone in rooms, in love / with our work" (69). The line break after "love" emphasizes the unexpected phrase "with our work." Although this marriage of true minds is romantic and sexual, their "work," their poetry, is a foundation for their relationship and their happiness.

Although Hacker's hedonism falls in the middle of the hedonistic spectrum, certain aspects of Epicureanism, such as delaying short-term gratification for long-term gain, are important to Hacker's hedonistic ethics (Feldman 94). Because Hacker is away in France and their relationship is in its nascent stages, fantasy and anticipation dominate the first two sections, as we can see in the speaker's fantasy of the two sharing a house and working in France in "Lacoste IV." The detailed imagined scenario—it being noon while the two, who have agreed not to speak until seven, work independently—mimics their actual physical separation by the Atlantic Ocean. The line, "Pleasure delayed is pleasure amplified," in the context of the poem refers both to the great pleasure it will be when they can speak to one another after their self-imposed vow of silence and to the satisfaction they will glean from patiently waiting until nightfall to eat the cassoulet (25). Moreover, in the context of their relationship, the line implies that waiting to engage in this type of cohabitation will make it all the more fulfilling; the reality will outshine the fantasy.

The concept of delayed pleasure being more satisfying can be applied to the sexual nature of their relationship. Although the beginning of the text frequently, often humorously, focuses on the topic of sexual desire—in "March Wind," for example, Hacker writes, "I almost came in my new herringbones / in the Via delgi Alfani, just / imagining your *socks* off"—the relationship between Hacker and Ray is not consummated until the third section (47). Although this delay is caused in part by Hacker's travels, there are also ethical concerns that postpone their actions, as we can see in "Lesbian Ethics, or; Live Girl-Girl Sex Acts." The speaker acknowledges her overwhelming desire for Ray, describes a previous daring sexual adventure in an airplane bathroom to prove to Ray that she's not "inimical to sleaze," but, because Ray is still involved with another woman, refuses to act on it because of infidelity's punning "bad taste" (6). Despite her longing, the speaker is willing to spend "precocious spring waiting on hold, in rut, / for clean time to be your low-minded lover" to truly enjoy their sexual relationship without guilt (6). This particular choice to delay pleasure in order to avoid the unpleasantness that would follow is in line with another key tenet of Epicureanism. In his "Letter to Menoeceus" Epicurus writes, pleasure is the starting-point and goal of living blessedly. For we recognized this as our first innate good, and this is our starting point for every choice and avoidance and we come to this by judging every good by the criterion of feeling. And it is just because this is the first innate good that we do not choose every pleasure; but sometimes we pass up many pleasures when we get a larger amount of what is uncongenial from them. (30)

Although Epicurus believes that pleasure is the good, he does not advocate indulging in every pleasure that presents itself because many pleasures, such as Hacker and Ray sleeping together before Ray ends her relationship with her previous serious partner, cause great pain in the long run. Additionally, Epicurus described the ethical relationship between pleasure and justice, as we can see in two of his maxims:

> V It is impossible to live pleasantly without living prudently, honourably, and justly and impossible to live prudently, honourably, and justly without living pleasantly. And whoever lacks this cannot live pleasantly.
> XVII The just life is most free from disturbance, but the unjust life is full of the greatest disturbance. (32–33)

One must lead a just life if one wants to be happy. Hacker's "lesbian ethics," here Epicurean, are hedonistic ethics, but due to her humorous delivery, she does not come across as preachy or priggish. In true hedonistic fashion, Hacker begins a sonnet about relationship ethics with a hilarious description of a past conquest, rhyming "getting it on" with "airplane john" in the process. Sex itself is not bad, and under the right circumstances it is good (and, it seems, in the case of the airplane bathroom, sometimes very good). It will not, however, be good or ultimately pleasurable if done under ethically questionable circumstances.

Hedonism has often been charged as immoral or amoral, but in reality, many types of hedonism adopt their own systems of morality. These systems are focused on situational ethical concerns, not prescribed morals. These ethical systems shift the onus of responsibility away from a governing body or a set of rules agreed upon by a majority and applied to all and toward the individual, creating a different societal model. In this type of system, although each person makes decisions based on his or her own pleasure, acting justly toward others is essential to acquiring happiness and living the good life.

Although there is plenty of Dionysian revelry—rich food, good wine, beautiful clothes, good sex—to be found throughout Hacker's text, this type of indulgence in pleasure is not figured as immoral or amoral. Rather, it is figured as good and as a central component of a good life, as the beginning of the poem "You, little one, are just the kind of boy" illustrates:

> You, little one, are just the kind of boy
> I would have eyeballed at the bar, and cruised
> efficiently, and taken home, and—used?
> Hell, no! The bodice busters say "enjoy" (17)

Hacker, with an emphatic, "Hell, no!" forcefully rejects the idea that taking someone back to her place and sleeping with that person upon first meeting is using them. She refigures this act as pleasurable by replacing "used" with the romance novel cliché "enjoy." Although eye-rollingly silly on one level, this substitution strips such actions of their negative, immoral connotations and shows them to be mutually pleasurable and comforting, leading them "to the place [they] both belong" (17).

At the end of the work, Ray and Hacker have ended their relationship, but Hacker has not abandoned her hedonistic paradigm. In the book's final poem "Did you love well what very soon you left?" Hacker writes, "the only gift / I got to keep or give is what I've cried" and laments "I drank our one year out in brine instead / of honey from the seasons of your tongue" (212). Although in her own words, "bereft," Hacker is still describing the world in hedonistic terms. Like drinking tears or brine, the end of their relationship is not pleasurable and is contrasted with the much more pleasing image of drinking honey from her lover's tongue. She has not changed her value system; the relationship has just stopped being a source of pleasure. Instead of slaking one's thirst, brine intensifies it, ending the book with an image of unquenched desire, which the speaker will eventually seek to fulfill with another lover.

By representing a pleasurable, and therefore good, life of a lesbian feminist, Hacker offers a critique of those who label her life as bad or immoral because of some agreed-upon social code. If one thinks that adhering to social standards constitutes a good life, then one is missing out on a good time. Hacker's hedonistic paradigm counters laws or proposals that marginalize people based on sexual orientation, gender, etc. From a hedonistic perspective, any law that does not promote people's happiness is not a just law. What makes someone happy depends, ultimately, on the individual. No government can prescribe a uniform way of life that yields the good life for everyone, and therefore, her work implies, governments should stay out of the business of regulating life choices.

Bursting at the Seams

Exploding the Confines of Reification with Creative Constraints in Harryette Mullen's *Sleeping with the Dictionary*

Rather than creating humorous narratives generated by the interplay of the particulars of contemporary autobiography and traditional, received poetic forms as Hacker does, Mullen often generates humor from nonnarrative word play, in which the words themselves are the source and focus of the humor. While Hacker expands the sonnet sequence by depicting a lesbian relationship, Harryette Mullen draws upon the tradition of poetic proceduralism to question the relationships between capitalism and discrimination. All the while, both poets seem to revel in the pleasures of language and engagement with poetic genre.

Mullen's poems in *Sleeping with the Dictionary* are playful yet mysterious. They seem to toy with the reader. For instance, the opening line of "Daisy Pearl," "More than a woman's name. Her traditional shape," reads like a riddle, challenging the reader to look closer for clues to figure it all out (18). The poem's language conjures images of sex, but many words allude to drinking, including "wedge" (of lime), "drunk," and "suck." By the time the reader reaches "Frozen / ones and fruity ones," most likely, he or she will think of margaritas. As it turns out, "margarita" is a woman's name, the Latin word for "pearl," and the Spanish word for "daisy," making the poem's title itself a clue (*Oxford English Dictionary Online*). As soon as the poem's subject and organizing principle are discovered, puns abound. "Diminutive," set off on its own as a single-word sentence in the third line is punning on the Spanish suffix "-ita," which can indicate that something is small; "stamina" in line four suggests the stamen of a flower, in this case a daisy, as well as the effect that one too many margaritas can have on sexual stamina; the reference to "on the border" plays on our associations with the border between the United States and Mexico; etc. At some point in the reader's ludic reverie, they will probably wonder why Mullen is playing games with her audience. One answer to that question, I suggest, may be found in yet another game: the crossword puzzle.

The crossword puzzle, according to *The Oxford Guide to Word Games*, "developed from the acrostic and the word square, but gained its popularity by combining elements of these games with cryptic clues which are similar to riddles" (57). The cryptic clues often rely upon word games and linguistic structures, such as anagrams, puns, and homophones (Augarde 67–69). These characteristics of crosswords can also be found in Mullen's *Sleeping with the Dictionary*. The poems employ creative constraints based upon the same chuckle- and/or groan-worthy word games, and the cryptic nature of the constraints invites, if not challenges, the reader to discover the structural principle with investigative skills not unlike those used to solve a clue's riddle.

The parallels between crosswords and Mullen's poems do not end with these shared linguistic features, though. When describing the types of clues commonly found in cryptic crosswords, Tony Augarde claims, "perhaps the best clues in cryptic crosswords are those that ingeniously use lateral thinking to devise new ways of looking at familiar words and phrases" (69). Mullen's poems, then, are similar to the best clues because, through the investigative process that the linguistic humor and the covert creative constraints engender, words and phrases are relearned (and sometimes unlearned), provoking in the reader a more complex understanding of the language that constructs their world. Beyond teaching readers to "avoid taking clues at face value," as cryptic crossword puzzles do, Mullen's work encourages readers not to take language at face value and to explore the sociopolitical ramifications of American English.

When comparing the form of crosswords to that of Mullen's poems, however, significant differences emerge. A crossword puzzle has a strict, determined structure and one fixed solution. Although each poem in *Sleeping with the Dictionary* has a creative constraint that helps to determine the poem's form, Mullen frequently bends rules, as we can see in her prose poem "sonnets" as well as her flexible use of Oulipian techniques.[1] In addition, the poems do not have a singular or neat solution. While discovering a poem's covert constraint can provide the reader with a richer understanding of that poem, the discovery often leads to multiple, complicated readings, exploding the confines of the arbitrary constraint, thus demonstrating the impossibility of containing language and the possibility of transcending imposed limits through innovation, at the level of both the word and the world.

Mullen's poems, though undoubtedly—at times indulgently—ludic, are staunchly socially engaged. They repeatedly invoke, enact, and lament the struggles of those who are oppressed in US society, especially women and African Americans. More importantly, though, Mullen's work explores the potential causes of this subjugation. One system that Mullen indicts as a disseminator and enforcer of this oppression is American capitalism. More specifically, many of Mullen's poems critique reification, a term first thoroughly explored by Georg Lukacs in *History and Class Consciousness* and aptly glossed by Timothy Bewes in his work *Reification, or the Anxiety of Late Capitalism*:

Reification refers to the moment that a process or relation is generalized into an abstraction, and thereby turned into a "thing." In Marxist theories of labour, reification is what happens when workers are installed in a place within the capitalist mode of production, and thus reduced to the status of a machine part. It is closely allied to the processes of alienation, objectification, and the fetishism of commodities, in which "the definite social relation between men themselves [assumes] the fantastic form of a relation between things." . . . In the broader socio-political sphere, reification is what happens in every instance of racism and sexism, where the objects of prejudice are perceived not as human beings but as things or "types." (3–4)

For the purposes of my analysis of Mullen's work, I am using "reification" to refer to the mental habits of forming static conceptions of the world and detaching from that world—these habits fueled by consumer culture. The reified relationship that consumer culture creates between people and the things they consume affects people's relationships to one another. Reification enables the subjugation of people since it allows one to see as "things" both other people and relationships between people.

The process of interrogating the poetic form of Mullen's poems to discover the creative constraint is analogous to interrogating societal structures and the reified conceptions that often order American society. At times Mullen experiments with and alters received forms, which, as Jessica Lewis Luck notes, enables her "to revel in the ludic pleasures of Oulipian constructions while maintaining at the same time an accessible, often political, theme" (365). By extension, I contend that by breaking out of the forms' constraints, Mullen encourages readers to reexamine and possibly break out of frozen conceptions of reality. Mullen's creative constraints demonstrate that inventiveness can spring from constraint, acting as a metaphor for the situation of oppressed peoples. Though constraints are imposed upon people because of their race, gender, religion, sexual orientation, etc., Mullen shows that constraint does not equal control or containment, since her formal constraints yield seemingly innumerable, uncontainable meanings. Mullen's use of humor is also integral to her critique of reified thought, since it helps to expose the absurd, skewed values of American society and the warped logic of reified thought. The different types and structures of humor that Mullen employs encourage readers to become aware of the negative effects of reification and to interrogate reified thought by causing moments of disruption in the text. The game-like poems in *Sleeping with the Dictionary* and the lateral thinking they demand from the reader make the process of reification visible, enabling the reader to recognize it, critique it, and, potentially, break out of its confines.

In this chapter I will examine five poems from *Sleeping with the Dictionary* in order to demonstrate the varied ways Mullen uses formal constraints and humor to expose the damaging effects that the process of reification has on oppressed peoples and to interrogate and critique the language that sustains their oppression. My readings of these poems also demonstrate the pervasiveness of the damage produced by reified thought since the poems reveal how it affects such disparate and fundamental areas of life as gender and race relations, religion, and romantic love.

Before examining these specific poems, a brief discussion of Mullen's poetic concerns is helpful in establishing the backdrop for the argument. Throughout *Sleeping with the Dictionary*, one can see Mullen's diverse poetic influences. Elisabeth Frost, Cynthia Hogue, and Juliana Spahr have convincingly traced Gertrude Stein's influence on Mullen's work,[2] and Mullen claims Umbra poet Lorenzo Thomas as a major influence (Mullen, "Poetry and Identity" 88). Her linguistic experimentation and questioning of subjectivity align her work with Language writers[3] (Frost, "Interview," paragraph 12), and her interest in African American voices resonates with writers of the Black Arts Movement. Aldon Lynn Nielsen attaches Mullen to a critically underrepresented and underappreciated tradition of African American experimentalist poets (Nielsen 35). These diverse influences make Mullen's work highly complex and highly resistant to labels as it foregrounds both "speakerly" and "writerly" aspects of language (Frost "Interview" paragraph 9).[4]

This fusion of "speakerly" and "writerly" language can be seen in Mullen's Oulipian-influenced, cryptographic writing. She discusses the possibilities of cryptography in an article on Sandra Cisneros's work. Mullen claims that "cryptic encodings of names and secret messages in the literary text privilege the literate over the illiterate, since they have no oral equivalent outside of literate discourses. Yet other encodings, while included in a literary discourse refer to the 'experience of the other' (Freire and Macado 12). This discourse of the other included illiteracy and orality, superstition and folk culture, ignorance and resistance" (Mullen, "Silence" 3). Mullen's use of covert constraints in her own poems is akin to these encodings. These constraints can be unsettling, causing the reader to feel like an outsider until he or she cracks the poem's proceduralist code. This process of cracking the code demands a high level of engagement from the reader. By encouraging readers to enter a state of deep engagement with the text, Mullen creates an atmosphere of interrogation. The heightened awareness that the reader must assume in order to engage with the poems impels readers to then question the poem's content, which makes this type of poetry an effective vehicle for encouraging empathy and questioning political conditions, such as the societal repression of marginalized peoples and the reified thinking that sustains that oppression.

These experiences of feeling like an insider or an outsider are related to Mullen's concerns with subjectivity, which can be seen in the structure of the book. The arrangement of the poems in *Sleeping with the Dictionary* is alphabetical. All the letters of the alphabet or represented by entries with the exceptions of "y" "u" and "i." These exceptions constitute a gesture of questioning conventional ideas about issues of identity since the homophones of the letters create the question, "Why you and I?" Mullen does not allow her poetic persona to be limited to a single subjectivity and recognizes that her readership is composed of individuals and is not easily reducible to a generic "you."[5] This refusal to limit subjectivity is a gesture that critiques reified thought, which often encourages people to think of others as objects or as easily definable things by severely limiting their subjectivities.[6]

These deliberate alphabetic exclusions can also be read as a comment upon how the dictionary encourages a more scientific/detached relationship with language. Words are collected, organized, and defined, but the dictionary does not address how words affect individuals in the context of their culture. Words become mere tools with defined functions, and their relationship to subjectivity and individual or group identity is abstracted. As Juliana Spahr claims,

> race is made absolute in linguistic reality in a way that it can never be in bodily reality. It is grammar that grants subjectivity. The "I" with its place as subject of the sentence can claim as a result of grammar's authorizing powers a substantive existence. This is not to deny the very real nonlinguistic results of oppression—bodily pain, for instance—but rather to suggest that attempts to counter oppression must also concentrate on claims made by linguistic authority. (91)

Spahr rightly asserts that Mullen's work illustrates that "the difficult and necessary work of challenging limiting subjectivities requires also that one challenge the strictures of grammar and rigorous narrative" (92). In *Sleeping with the Dictionary*, Mullen's elaborate word play focuses this challenge on individual words to question the idea that words, which are the building blocks for grammar and narrative, are static objects bound by strict rules removed from the makeup of one's subjectivity. This challenge at the level of the word implies that in order to challenge reified thought processes, we must start at the foundation with the building blocks of language.

Mullen's lengthy poem "Jingle Jangle" is a prime example of how she challenges the reader to think about the functions of words by highlighting the nonsemantic properties of language. The poem revels in the pleasure that the sounds of language create. The poem is composed of the jingles, the background noise that American culture hears daily, the words and phrases that jangle around in our minds. The constraints on the poem are that it is an abecedarian, a poem whose form is determined by the alphabet ("Abecedarius"), and that the entries are alliterative or rhyming words and phrases themselves arranged, with a few exceptions, in alphabetical order, as can be seen in the letter 'd' section:

> date rape deadhead deep sleep dikes on bikes dilly-dally
>   ding-a-ling ding-dang dingle-dangle
> ding-dong dirty birdy Dizzy Lizzie dog log Don Juan. (*SWTD* 32)

In his work *Puns*, Walter Redfern seeks to explain why people find rhyming words and other words associated by similar sounds humorous: "On the most passive level, 'there is pleasure in phonetic free association not unlike the joys of daydreaming.' The associative rhyme clearly revels in similarities, recurrences, echoes, reminders, assonances and rhymes. Perhaps we revel so much because we are not supposed to" (11). Taking pleasure in the sounds of words detracts from the way that we are "supposed" to use language, i.e., for communication. Though it would be easy to read this poem for the pure enjoyment of its play with sound, as Warren F. Motte Jr. observes about the Oulipo's work, "serious and playful intent are not mutually exclusive." In Mullen's work, I argue, "they are, on the contrary, insistently and reciprocally implicative" (Motte 21). In "Jingle Jangle," many of the terms are gleaned from the advertisements that inundate our consciousness ("Osh Kosh B'Gosh"). Others come from slang: "fried, dyed, laid to the side." Some entries seem merely empty and senseless, like children's rhymes ("dingle-dangle"), yet many of the entries are politically charged. Several terms denote violence ("date rape") and others are discriminatory and as such enact a kind of violence ("Jew Canoe," "hairy fairy," "dikes on bikes," "nig nog," "jig rig"). By placing these terms in a silly-sounding poem, their violence is even more troubling as the phonetic qualities of the terms contribute to the fun of the poem.

What Mullen's poem emphasizes is that language, and the way language can be "packaged," fuels and facilitates consumerism. It shows how the humorous, nonsemantic aspects help to sell products and that humorous product names are more effective at selling products than accurate descriptions of the products. Language in effect becomes reified, a product that is bought and sold. Though this packaging of language may be used in relatively innocuous tasks, such as marketing food, the poem shows that this packaging is also used for such damaging ends as objectifying women and disseminating cultural stereotypes.

As Mullen's collection of jingles demonstrates, the packaging of the product's name is as essential for successful marketing as its physical packaging. The title of the poem contains "jingle" which, though it denotes sound in an onomatopoetic way (as in the song "Jingle Bells"), it also references the catchy slogan of an advertising campaign, often set to music, with the purpose of encouraging consumers to purchase a product. As noted above, many of the phrases included in the poem are from ads or product names, such as "Ronald McDonald," "Chubby Hubby," "Chunky Monkey," "Kit Kat," "Crunch and Munch," "Mac Attack," "Shake 'n Bake," and "Shedd's Spread." Indeed, these examples from ads and product names illustrate that the sounds of language appeal to consumers through rhyme and alliteration. Also, since rhyme and alliteration are memorable, these names and slogans are more likely to be remembered by consumers, a phenomenon explained by the "bathtub effect": "In psycholinguistics, the 'bathtub effect' is the colorful term used to indicate that the beginning and end of a word have a naturally salient status" (Attardo, *Humorous Texts*, 91). As an additional form of appeal, some of these product names conjure up humorous images. On first encounter, the images of an overweight primate and a portly spouse generated by "Chunky Monkey" and "Chubby Hubby" undoubtedly elicit chuckles from many consumers, attracting their attention and encouraging them to add the products to their shopping carts. The numerous examples of these rhyming, alliterative, and/or humorous product names illustrate advertisers often persuade people to consume because of the product's name, rather than its inherent merit. This tendency demonstrates that people can be affected and persuaded by the nonsemantic aspects of language as much as, or maybe more than, they are by the literal meanings of the words. This idea is illustrated by the fact that the above product names, such as "Chunky Monkey" and "Crunch and Munch," do not identify what the product actually is. In addition, these product names reference food or restaurants, which emphasizes the link among cultural consumption, physical consumption in these instances, and language.

Though these commercial product names are the most obvious representation of how reified thought can transform words into commodities in the poem, other terms illustrate how reification encourages the objectification of women. Several of the terms in the poem are slang for women's body parts, such as "fur burger" (36) that demean a woman's body, making her body or body parts seem like objects to be laughed at. Other terms, such as "hump & dump" (37) and "pump & dump" (40) refer to having sex with a woman and tossing her aside like trash, using her body and throwing it away, making women seem like disposable products that are essentially the same and easily replaceable. Though actions such as these are harmful and heartless, the funny-sounding terms, while crude in nature, function like euphemisms in that they distract from the gravity of the actions. These examples of objectifying women lead to terms for even more violent acts, such as "date rape" and "gang bang." The process of objectifying women's bodies, which reified thought encourages, is associated with sexually violent crimes against women since women are portrayed as sex objects and objectification helps legitimize abuse.

The fact that the term "gang bang" follows directly after "gal pal" is striking since the words have such different tones, one being so innocent and the other so violent. As Mullen stated in an interview when speaking of her book, *Muse & Drudge*, "You can also heighten paradox and contradiction when you compress together things that come from very different registers or lexicons; they jostle each other so there's more tension. Yet there's more elasticity in the utterance" (Bedient 656–57). This idea of heightening contradiction via compression is equally applicable to this poem. Though these terms seem to come from different lexicons, the proximity of the terms, due to the constraints of the form, invites comparison and connection. Through this comparison one can surmise that the process of reification facilitates someone's "gal pal" becoming the victim of a "gang bang," or rape by multiple men, since she may be viewed primarily as a sexual object by the perpetrators. The violence of "gang bang" is heightened by the proximity of "gal pal," because of the latter term's connotations of personal intimacy.

Mullen's poem, by emphasizing the phonetic qualities of language, indicates that derogatory terms may be perpetuated because of the way they sound—the way they are "packaged." Just as advertisers use rhyming and alliterative product names and slogans, the humorous aspects of language are also used to "sell" racism and sexism. There are many discriminatory terms in American English, but some of the terms Mullen selects are particularly harmful because they sound funny. This humor allows people to gloss over the violence embedded in these terms in a way that other derogatory terms, which do not rhyme or sound silly, cannot. "Jangle," the second word in the poem's title, has connotations of being snarled or mixed up. Though the idea of the poem as a jangle speaks to the collection of words and phrases from disparate lexicons (slang, advertisements, etc.), it also refers to the way that the sounds of language can draw our attention away from the literal meaning of something. When analyzing "Jingle Jangle" and other poems from *Sleeping with the Dictionary* with similar forms, Alan Gilbert argues that, "in the extreme form of leveling that these pieces perform (where 'multi-culti' is the same as 'mumbo jumbo'), linguistic—and, by implication, social—hierarchies are assailed" (59). Although I agree that the poem enacts a form of social leveling through the juxtaposition of different registers of language, I think that Mullen is also indicating how language can be manipulated to perpetuate and sustain social hierarchies. One way of reading the poem is to focus on and revel in the sounds of its language. The sounds are fun and funny, but this play causes the reader to ignore the meaning of the terms used in the poem. By putting a racial slur in humorous packaging, the slur can seem less offensive. However, this packaging is more dangerous as it encourages people to accept or tolerate these terms and by extension the derogatory ideas underneath the attractive wrapping. In "Race and Ethnicity and Popular Humor," Dennis Howitt and Kwame Owusu-Bempah argue "that jokes are bound by social rules which, when not followed, can cause problematic social exchanges" (46). Refusing to laugh at or accept a racist joke breaks these social rules (47). Therefore, these social rules make jokes and humorous phrases effective vehicles for spreading discrimination. As Howitt and Owusu-Bempah argue, "Jokes are communicative acts which play a significant role in social exchanges—a medium through which society disseminates and generationally transmits its dominant attitudes toward outgroups. Racist jokes, therefore, act as propaganda in support of racist ideology" (49). Although Howitt and Owusu-Bempah focus on racist jokes, discriminatory jokes in general can be seen as propaganda in support of discriminatory ideologies. In a similar fashion, I argue, the poem enacts the way that by manipulating the humorous, phonetic possibilities of language, the dominant culture can disseminate stereotypes and cultural myths via supposedly playful language. For example, the phrases "Jew canoe" and "jig rig," which are located next to one another in the poem, are two terms that stereotype the kinds of cars that Jewish Americans and African Americans drive. A "Jew canoe" is slang for a long car, such as a Cadillac, that Jewish Americans supposedly drive, while a "jig rig" describes a dilapidated car that an African American, especially one who is poor, drives (*Dictionary of Slang*). "Jig" is a racial slur against African Americans and "rig" implies that something was put together in a haphazard manner. Both of these terms are damaging, but because they rhyme, they contribute to the fun of the poem, which is especially disturbing. Other harmful phrases which contribute to the fun of the poem are "nig-nog" and "fag hag," the former a racial slur against African Americans and the latter a slur against homosexuals, especially homosexual men, and the women who befriend them (*Oxford Dictionary of Modern Slang*). By emphasizing the phonetic properties of language and using juxtaposition, Mullen exposes how damaging phrases and ideas packaged in humorous sounds can be disseminated in a way that other derogatory terms without these phonetic properties cannot. The detachment from the world fueled by reified thought facilitates the disconnection between a funny-sounding phrase and the gravity of its meaning. The phrase becomes an aesthetic object detached from its meaning and, more importantly, its effects on individuals and cultural consciousness. Howitt and Owusu-Bempah argue that racist jokes "continually reinforce the use of race categories in our thinking" (62). Expanding upon this claim, I contend that the humorous-sounding derogatory terms cited above, whether racist, sexist, homophobic, etc., reify derogatory ideas about groups of people, placing people into artificial categories. Although Mullen uses humor to show how these racist and violent terms are a part of American cultural consciousness, she also reveals that humor can be manipulated to help package and sell these terms.

As stated above, the form of the poem is an abecedarian. Though abecedarians have been written by many serious poets, they have also been used as mnemonic devices to teach children the alphabet and properties of language. In a sense, Mullen is using this abecedarian to instruct (or at least remind) her readers about the properties of language, too, especially how its phonetic qualities can generate humor and how that humor can persuade and encourage acceptance of damaging ideas. Abecedarians have a long tradition and have been seen as powerful "since in the a[becedarian] the master code of the lang[uage] is made the constitutive device of the form" ("Abecedarius"). Mullen harnesses this power in order to show readers the pervasiveness of the violence of American English. The poem includes some type of slur or derogatory term for nearly every letter of the alphabet. In addition, the restrictions and compression of the poem allow for surprising and often disturbing juxtapositions of terms and ideas, lending the humor of the poem an uncomfortable valence, which encourages interrogation of the poem's language and, by extension, interrogation of the culture constructed and sustained by that language.

While "Jingle Jangle" demonstrates how the phonetic qualities of language can be manipulated in order to sustain oppression, "The Lunar Lutheran" uses anagrams to expose the constructedness of religious identities and the violence and corruption, especially economic corruption, often accompanying religion (Mullen, "Sleeping" 48). The poem indicates how reified thought has caused institutionalized religion to become commodified and how many religions have histories of commodifying others. Anagrams highlight the materiality of language. By interchanging the letters of words, Mullen connects different religions linguistically in "The Lunar Lutheran." This linguistic connection implies that these religions are made from the same material and are, to an extent, interchangeable. Mullen's poem shows us that this interchangeability goes beyond linguistic construction to the widespread economic corruption of religions. Because of this corruption, the religions are represented as quite similar in that they are all for sale. As we will see, the humor is generated in part by the seeming oddity of grouping: sex, yoga, Mormonism, Buddhism, and Hollywood.[7] The fact that these associations are humorous due to their seeming incongruity demonstrates that religions function as static structures removed from the system of capitalism. Mullen is showing that religions as institutions and capitalism are not separable, but interdependent, de-reifying thoughts about religion as a structure removed from—or immune to—economic corruption.

Before delving into an examination of how Mullen's anagrammatic work critiques religious groups in "The Lunar Lutheran," it will prove useful to explore the history of the anagram, especially its use in English language and literature, in order to see how Mullen alters or adopts conventional uses. In "On the Anagram and Its Functions," Karel Bares provides a detailed study of the anagram and its history. She notes that the anagram, which owes its existence to graphics, classically involves a complete inversion of the sequence of letters of the base word (141). Bares claims that the diverse reasons for using anagrams throughout history include demonstrating one's good education; conveying praise; displaying wit or peculiarity; offering an attack, gallant flattery, cryptic coding, tomb inscription, political allusion; and providing name brands of products and advertising (a recent example of the last is a Toyota CAMRY commercial which rearranges the words MY CAR into CAMRY) (144–47). According to *The Oxford Guide to Word Games*, which discusses the anagram's historical impact in varied languages, Cabbalists believed that there were magical properties in the Hebrew alphabet and that the letters used in sacred Jewish writing could be rearranged to work miracles and reveal truth (Augarde 80). Anagrams of names often were believed to foretell one's future (Augarde 81). These diverse examples all involve repossession and refiguring of language in order to achieve a desired end.

This brief, by no means comprehensive, history of the anagram helps us to engage with Mullen's work. Mullen foregrounds the graphic nature of language in the poems' encodings, which the anagram helps her to do. The anagram's long association with naming resonates in Mullen's concerns with language and identity and with the constructed and prescribed nature of both. As Bares asserts, "in an anagram the thoughts of discovering and disclosing something hidden, on the one hand, and of veiling and hiding something one the other hand, are dialectically combined" (151). Mullen utilizes these properties of the anagram in order to address issues of identity, especially the antiessentialist "mongrel" identity that she discussed in an interview with Calvin Bedient about her earlier work *Muse and Drudge*:

> A lot has been said of how American culture is a miscegenated culture, how it is a product of a mixing and a mingling of diverse races and cultures and languages, and I would agree with that. I would say that, yes, my text is deliberately a multi-voiced text, a text that tries to express the actual diversity of my own experience living here, exposed to different cultures. "Mongrel" comes from "among." Among others. We are among; we are not alone. We are all mongrels. (652)

Mullen's anagrams demonstrate the interconnectedness of words and of the people who use them. Just as anagrams allow us to see words as mongrels, as constructions made from a mixture of letters or even of languages, so too do they enable us to see people as mongrels who influence one another. This antiessentialist conception of identity helps to combat racist, sexist, and other reductive reified thought in which "the objects of prejudice are perceived not as human beings but as things or 'types'" (Bewes 4).

Mullen's anagrams demonstrate the interrelations within language: that a word may contain other words and may be constructed from others, that these other words are coded into the words we encounter, and that their presence can and should affect the way we read and interpret the world. Though this process is similar to etymology in that it demonstrates relationships between words, it is not as restrictive, allowing for phonetic and visual connections. While the reader (and, presumably, the writer) gleans a great deal of enjoyment from the play with language and the often-humorous connections that Mullen's anagrammatic poems encourage the reader to make, the principles of fracture, rearrangement, and reconstruction inherent to the anagram represent both the violence and the redeeming power that language possesses. Mullen reveals that the tasks of reading and decoding meaning, which everyone faces daily, are daunting. In *Sleeping with the Dictionary*, the poems that utilize the anagram do not adhere to a definite structure, and they do not explicitly declare that anagrams are a structural device. Instead, Mullen's anagrammatic play encourages the reader to interrogate the text in order to discover the organizational forces at work behind the poems and behind language in general. Mullen's language play is empowering, a repossession of language which allows her to explore and interrogate identity as it is constructed in the real world and in the world of the poem. Yet, her covert linguistic coding can also alienate the reader, making them feel marginalized and manipulated by the poems' cryptographic nature. At the same time, Mullen's coded poems encourage readers to adopt new reading techniques, lending them freedom to explore the poems' language for many levels of meaning, pleasure, and challenge. Both the exclusion and empowerment that the reader experiences from Mullen's anagrams demonstrate by extension both the limitations that prescribed identities place upon an individual and the available liberation of self-exploration and self-definition.[8]

In "The Lunar Lutheran" Mullen uses humor and anagrams to show the constructedness of religious identities as well as the similarities and differences among religious groups. She verbally slides one religion into another, encouraging a more fluid, rather than denominational, understanding of spirituality. In addition to troubling the boundaries among religious groups, Mullen humorously weaves in images from popular culture in order to show that religion does not exist in a vacuum and to indicate how religion and capitalist society overlap and conflict. There is obvious playfulness inherent in lines such as, "I heard this from a goy who taught yoga in the home of Goya" (48). This play with language creates some surprising yet deliberate overlapping among religious groups and spiritual beliefs. The opening lines declare that a "Pisces pal" is "a friend to all Episcopals." Mullen's anagrams linguistically connect these figures but also imply that people who believe in astrology associate with or may even identify themselves as Episcopalian. Roman Catholics and Mormons are linked anagrammatically and thematically by a description of a woman engaging in a more Eastern, meditative spiritual activity (saying "Om"), troubling (or de-reifying) essentialist religious identification. Mullen's humor also encourages readers to interpret this meditative practice of humming "Om" as a sexual act since Mullen writes, "Mom hums 'Om' with no other man than Norm or Ron" (48). The anagrammatic association between "Mom" and *Roman* Catholics and *Mormons* connects Mom's sexual promiscuity to members of both religions, reminding readers that people who consider themselves to be devout followers of these religions may also transgress the rules of those religions. Sometimes the anagrams seem rather nonsensical, such as "Oh tears oxen trod!" which is an anagram of "orthodox Easter." Yet the process of creating this anagram deliberately scrambles the notion of "orthodox" itself. Mullen's anagrams also connect Hollywood to established religious groups: "His Buddhist robe hid this budding D bust in this B movie dud." This connection encourages readers to see Hollywood as its own type of religion, replete with millions of devout followers, and to recognize that Hollywood's influence on the public may be as powerful as that of any religion.

The tensions created by the blending of one faith into another via anagrammatic play also have a grim side. Images of violence as well as references to money lead the reader to think of the corruption of institutions of faith as well as violence between different faiths. The negative influence of reified thought upon religion can be seen in the question, "What would it cost to gain the soul of an agnostic?" which is bitingly funny due to its economically inflected diction. The mention of purchasing someone's soul indicates that the history of many religious institutions is riddled with economic corruption that persists to the present day, but, more importantly, the question shows the influence of reified thought, as the purchase of a soul turns it into a thing, a commodity. In Timothy Bewes's work *Reification* he states, "Christian redemption is the promise of a nonworldly, thus, nonreified existence; it is structurally analogous to the Marxist promise of revolution but projected in a metaphysical form that is categorically removed from the worldly activity of politics" (Bewes 5). However, Mullen's question and its undertone of buying and selling souls indicates that, in actuality, religious redemption is anything but "categorically removed" from the secular market economy. Thus, the economic corruption of religious institutions corrupts the beliefs and promises that those institutions represent. The closing lines of the poem allude to these issues of money and violence most explicitly with the words "hate" and "heist" and the image of "stab[bing] a pit bull." Though the groups mentioned are Muslims, agnostics, atheists, Baptists, and Hindus, the reader has the sense that these specific groups are not the only ones associated with corruption but that these issues can be associated with all religious—or antireligious—groups. As Mullen has shown through her anagrammatic play, these groups are not as separable as one may have thought.

In addition, recalling the Cabbalist notions that anagrams can lead to revelation of truths, Mullen's anagrams reenvision relations between religious groups, possibly troubling readers' received understandings of these relationships. This language play could also be a critique of those religions that treat religious texts as static objects/artifacts, limiting personal interpretation and spiritual exploration to the purposes of solidarity and agreement upon spiritual beliefs. She demonstrates a reprocessing of language in order to question essentialist notions of religious identity and difference.

In the same year that *Sleeping with the Dictionary* was published, another African American poet published a book featuring anagrammatic play as a means of exploring identity issues. In *Hip Logic* Terrance Hayes entitles two of the five sections "A Gram of &s," featuring procedural anagrammatic poems that work to decode familiar terms in order to revise and question the relationship between language and identity. In a 2004 interview, Hayes states that as a poet he is interested in "how language can be worn and changed," as his anagrammatic poems demonstrate ("The Poet"). Hayes foregrounds his form and process by explaining the origin and format of his anagrammatic form in the endnotes to his book, *Hip Logic*:

> The poems are based on the daily word game found in the puzzle section of many syndicated newspapers. I end each line with one of the eleven words derived from the title word, while abiding by the other rules of the game: 1. Words must be derived from four or more letters. 2. Words that acquire four letters by the addition of "s," such as "bats" or "dies" are not used. 3. Only one form of a verb is used. (91)

Hayes's highly structured anagrammatic poems, which adopt the title base word as a thematic and structural device, demonstrate a high level of language's communicability, even when under such restrictive formal constraints. As McRae claims in *Lyric as Comedy: The Poetics of Abjection in Postwar America*, "Hayes is interested in form as a liberating constriction." One senses the desire of these poems to communicate and often redefine or explore the meanings of terms in spite of formal constraints in Hayes's inventive, gymnastic syntactic structures and creative line breaks, exhibiting the innovation necessary to effectively communicate under such conditions. Metonymically, these restrictive anagrammatic poems can be read as the struggle for people to question and potentially redefine their societally prescribed identity. Alternatively, Terrance Hayes's anagrammatic poems work to decode and deconstruct individual words in order to question prescribed and generally accepted notions about definitions of words and identities.

Though Hayes's anagrammatic poems are less subtle about their structural procedure than Mullen's, they are no less powerful; they raise questions about how language can contain and mask violence and promote ideas about identity that are difficult to dismantle, especially ideas concerning gender and race. The poems in these sections are arranged alphabetically by the title root word, reminiscent of the structure of a dictionary and of Mullen's book, making Hayes's attempts to explore and redefine these words all the more evident. The violent images in the poem "masculine," including "the mean / streak in your father's work belt" trace the association of violence and masculinity back to the Biblical story of creation, even implicating God "Himself" using the capitalized form, asserting patriarchal importance and reverence (63). The near-sacrilegious image of "old deacons" smiling at church reenactments of Mary Magdalene's supplicant action "to clean / the feet of Jesus to beat a stint in hell" acquires an even more disturbing note as one reads the closing image, which relegates the difference of males and females to a mere "gram of vein & muscle" (63).

The poem's meditation on the construction of masculine identity as dominant and males' abuse and love of power is heightened by its formal construction, which highlights the materiality of language and its fabricated nature. Hayes's construction of this poem around words derived anagrammatically from the title is analogous to the way ideas about masculinity are disseminated in society. The opening lines, "The word some dudes claim came / first," complicate the question of whether these violent tendencies are physiologically inherent to males or whether these characteristics were created and perpetuated by "the word" (63). At the same time that Hayes addresses the constructedness of language and gender roles, he also invokes the question of nature's role in the creation of identity. Just as the eleven words that end each line naturally derive from the base word, the reader is asked to question if the violence discussed in the poem is natural or inherent to maleness. As we saw in Mullen's anagrammatic work, Hayes utilizes the compression inherent to the anagram. Hayes decompresses the base word anagrammatically in order to expand/question our notions of the base word as both a linguistic and identity construct. This process of redefining, though restricted by the possible anagrams that the root word can produce, allows Hayes to explore the word in a manner free from etymological constraints and prescribed definitions.

Hayes and Mullen encourage the reader to perform linguistic excavation through their use of the anagram. Though their anagrammatic explorations are related to more conventional language study, such as etymology, their techniques suggest that these more conventional understandings of language are not comprehensive and are often limiting. Their poems' mutual engagement with the dictionary and with identity issues comments on the importance of refusing categorization and labeling in order to define the self through exploration of language, society, the individual, and the connections between them.

In addition to using poetic forms and word play, such as the abecedarian and anagrams, to explore relationships between language and identity formation, in "European Folktale Variant," Mullen rewrites the fairy tale "Goldilocks and the Three Bears" in a parody of the language of sensationalized media crime reports, in order to demonstrate how such stories are detached from the reality of criminalized racial groups. Here Mullen is attempting to respond to the world as it is for many people by exposing the absurdity of the fairy tale. By recasting Goldilocks as a criminal/victim, Mullen highlights how property is often valued above human life in the United States, especially when that life belongs to a member of a criminalized group. By making Goldilocks, a figure often connected with innocence since she is a child protagonist in a fairy tale, a criminal and silencing her, Mullen encourages people to question crime reports and to think of the person behind the crime. Undoubtedly the humor and absurdity of this version of the fairy tale is due partly to Goldilocks's whiteness. Though thinking of a character from a fairy tale as a criminal is absurd, this absurdity is also generated by the fact that Goldilocks is a white, blonde girl, a figure long associated with innocence. This association is still evident in contemporary media, as a recent study on the television show *Law & Order: Special Victims Unit* demonstrates. The study concludes, "almost two-thirds of 'SVU' victims are white. This over-representation connects whiteness with innocence and exploitation" (Britto et al. 14). Therefore, the humor generated by casting the white, blonde girl as a criminal exposes reified conceptions of whiteness. This connection of whiteness with innocence is an example of reified thought, since innocence is not determined in many people's minds on a case-by-case basis but is rather predetermined by turning whiteness into a "thing" associated with innocence and propriety.

Mullen's detailed description of Goldilocks's break-in is undoubtedly humorous: "a trespassing pre-teen / barged into the rustic country cottage of a nuclear family of / anthropomorphic bruins" (*SWTD* 24). Throughout the poem the humor stems, in part, from the translation of the children's story into the dramatic, legally inflected language of a piece of sensationalist crime journalism. In other words, the humor can be described as "register humor," which is "humor caused by an incongruity originating in the clash between two registers" (Attardo 230). The clash in the levels of diction between the original tale's "three bears" and

Mullen's "nuclear family of / anthropomorphic bruins" makes us laugh and thwarts our expectations. The innocence of this fairy tale is eradicated by the reinterpretation of Goldilocks's actions as criminal. The most glaring example of this transformation of innocence occurs as Mullen details Goldilocks's fate:

> With the assistance of the neighborhood crime patrol, law enforcement officers were able to apprehend and incarcerate the callow miscreant, who has been sentenced to juvenile detention. (*SWTD* 24–25)

The conventional version of the story ends with Goldilocks running out of the bears' abode after being discovered by them upon their return. The fact that Mullen's version ends with Goldilocks in juvenile detention shows that in our contemporary world, especially for members of criminalized minorities, the innocent Goldilocks tale is defunct. The humor of Goldilocks, the young white girl, as a criminal becomes disconcerting as the reader discerns the societal prejudices that generate it, making it, in Ron Jenkins's terms, "subversive." In his work, *Subversive Laughter*, he distinguishes between subversive American humor and "comedy of detachment." The detached comedy "dilutes the urgency of [the] comic themes" while subversive humor "unsettles the audience into an awareness that something is wrong" (Jenkins 180). Instead of pacifying the reader with detached humor, Mullen's clever, subversive humor challenges the reader to examine the racism that helps to create it.

Mullen's subversively funny revision of the fairy tale unsettles the reader by challenging and playing upon expectations of the familiar genre, one of which is the moral of the tale. In "Goldilocks and the Three Bears," the moral message is to caution little girls against curiosity and wandering off alone. Marina Warner, in *From the Beast to the Blonde*, analyzes fairy tales, including "Goldilocks," that dissuade children from engaging in improper behavior: "fairy tales are stories to frighten children, as well as delight them" (243). In a sense, Mullen's revised version more accurately instructs children, especially those of criminalized minorities, about the consequences of such behavior in contemporary American society.

This retelling of the tale of a blonde girl reveals how traditional European-derived fairy tales do not translate when applied to criminalized minorities. Significantly, in Mullen's reportorial version of the Goldilocks story, Goldilocks herself is robbed of her voice. One of the most important features of the traditional Goldilocks tale is Goldilocks's repeated evaluation of the porridge, the beds, etc., which all end in her declaration of "this one is just right." In Mullen's version, the reader has no direct relationship with Goldilocks at all. Everything is mediated through the poet as reporter. Most importantly, the reporter/speaker is extremely speculative: "Her motivation? Who can be sure? Some say the youthful offender was an innocent maiden who lost her sense of direction in the lush growth of the virgin pine forest. Or perhaps the elders of her tribe had neglected to attend to her proper socialization. In any case, this flaxen-haired vixen perpetrated a 'B and E,' a felony punishable by law" (*SWTD* 24). This type of speculation encourages readers to form their own opinions about Goldilocks without ever hearing her side of the story. The loaded descriptions of Goldilocks, such as "incorrigible pre-adolescent" and "puerile hoodlum," are reminiscent of the newspaper descriptions of Bigger Thomas in Richard Wright's *Native Son*. Bigger is described as a "jungle beast" among other derogatory slurs, which rob him of his humanity and in effect convict him before his trial (279). It is important to note that Goldilocks is a different species than the bears, which implies that criminals and criminalized people are seen as something other than human, just as Bigger Thomas was depicted. Goldilocks, too, is depicted as a criminal, and her actions define her. By rewriting Goldilocks, a character so ingrained in Western culture, as a criminal, Mullen is able to show how one-sided criminal reports are, how they conceal the humanity of the accused, and how they encourage readers to keep their minds closed and convict without ever thinking of the perspective of the person behind the crimes. Though this tale could reveal how people, in general, accused of crimes are robbed of their humanity, it specifically shows how European folktales inadequately portray reality for people criminalized because of their race. This rewriting of the tale reveals how "Goldilocks and the Three Bears" would sound if Goldilocks were treated as a child of a criminalized minority group.

The updated ending of the poem stresses the skewed values of a capitalist society in which property is valued above human life. The last lines demonstrate that society does not take responsibility for its criminals, but rather places the blame back onto the criminals and their families. The speaker states that lawyers for the bear family

> have filed suit against the criminally negligent parents of the wayward youth, and expect that the bruins will be awarded a substantial sum for emotional distress as well as for extensive damage to their property. (*SWTD* 25)

The youth's parents are held responsible, and all we know of them is that they are "criminally negligent." Blaming the parents or family of the criminal is common in our society. It is more common to hear the question "Where were their parents?" than "How did society fail this person?" In addition to blaming instead of determining the source of the problem, the poem shows American society's concern for material things. The traditional version of the story ends with Goldilocks fleeing the bears, but this version ends with a description of an impending lawsuit against the child's parents for "emotional distress as well as for extensive damage to their property." It is fitting that "property" is the final word of the poem, since concern for property catalyzes the response to and treatment of the girl.

In addition to rewriting fairy tales to highlight the criminalization of particular racial and ethnic groups, Mullen explores concerns about modern love through her rewrites of the traditional love sonnet. In both "Variation on a Theme Park" and "Dim Lady," Mullen uses the Oulipian technique of S + 7 to rewrite Shakespeare's "Sonnet 130" in order to critique how reified thought, encouraged and sustained by consumer culture, facilitates views of women and romantic love as objects or commodities. Oulipo, or Ouvroir de Littérature Potentielle, refers to a group of writers, mathematicians, and other intellectuals formed in 1960 dedicated to researching and inventing literary forms (Motte 1). The humor, which is generated in part by the difference between the linguistic registers of Shakespeare's and Mullen's poems, emphasizes how love has become corrupted by capitalist values. The form itself emphasizes words as replaceable objects, since S + 7, as I will explain in a moment, is predicated upon the substitution of words, and Mullen's substituted words describe the processes of economic exchange and objects that can be bought and sold. This act of replacement implies that the subject of Shakespeare's poem, no longer a unique, cherished individual, becomes replaceable in contemporary commodity culture, which again demonstrates the negative effects of reified thinking on relationships between people and on concepts of love.

Mullen's rewriting of Shakespeare's "Sonnet 130," "Variation on a Theme Park," suggests that the subject of Shakespeare's poem, love, is overshadowed by capitalism in contemporary American society. The poem replaces Shakespeare's famous first line "My mistress' eyes are nothing like the sun" with "My Mickey Mouse ears are nothing like sonar" (*SWTD* 75). Immediately, Mullen transforms this love poem into a poem about a commercialized image. This transformation is aided by Mullen's adaptation of the

S + 7 technique, which was invented by the Oulipo group. Raymond Queneau describes the S + 7 method in "Potential Literature":

> It consists in taking a text and replacing each substantive with the seventh following it in the dictionary. The result obviously depends on the dictionary one chooses. Naturally, the number seven is arbitrary. . . .
>
> One will notice that if the inverse of haikuization is the set rhyme, the inverse of S + 7 is cryptography (or, at least a chapter of cryptography): given a text treated by this method, find the original. (Motte 61)

In a note on the same piece on isomorphisms, Motte writes,

> the efficacy of translations of this sort depends largely on the shock they produce as they run into the original: that is, the reader must ideally "hear" the original and the transformation simultaneously, and the latter must jar the former (this is also true of the S + 7 Method). To produce this effect, the *untransformed* part of the new text . . . must follow the original faithfully. (Motte 189)

Though some of Mullen's substitutions seem to be chosen rather than mathematically discovered, the principle associated with the S + 7 technique that the reader should "hear" the original text and that "the latter must jar the former" is central to this poem's critique and its humor. Rewriting the love poem as a poem about a cartoon mouse is immediately humorous due to the incongruity inherent in the bizarre contrast with the original.

Mullen's rewriting of the first line also plays with the blazon, "a poetic genre devoted to the praise or blame of something" ("Blason"). The blazon has been indicted as violently dismembering women into body parts (141–42), and Mullen's "Mickey Mouse ears" play on that critique as the ears, sold at Disney theme parks, are a dismembering of Mickey. The word "her" in Shakespeare's sonnet is replaced with "Walt's," replacing Mickey's personal pronoun with the possessive form of his creator's name, showing the relationship between the man and the character that catalyzed his empire, making them seem almost interchangeable, as well as associating Walt Disney, a paragon of capitalism, with ownership and possession. This emphasis on ownership and possession is present throughout the poem, as can be seen in Mullen's economically inflected substitutions: "Wonder Bras" for "wires," "checkbook" for "cheeks," "purchases" for "perfumes," "bargains" for "breath," "bought" for "belied," and "coupons" for "compare" (*SWTD* 75). Mullen's version suggests that substance has been replaced with superficiality, love with consumerism. Mullen's poem even replaces "heav'n" with "halogen-light," indicating that religious faith has been replaced by commercialism. Most importantly, "love" has transformed into "loneliness," suggesting that a society obsessed with material goods instead of love is a sad, lonely, loveless society.

Several critics of Shakespeare's "Sonnet 130" critique the blazon and its tendency to objectify women,[9] and while "Dim Lady" seemingly tries to echo Shakespeare's version, it actually reinforces the commodification of women and, by extension, shows how a society obsessed with consumerism encourages that commodification. This poem is much closer to the original than was "Variation on a Theme Park." It keeps the sense of the poem but replaces the original words with more modern diction. In this example, "mistress" is replaced by slang terms for a lover, such as "honeybunch," "main squeeze," and "ball and chain" (*SWTD* 20). Most interesting are the substitutions Mullen makes for the words used to compare the mistress's body parts: "Today's special at Red Lobster" for "coral," "Liquid Paper" for "snow," "Slinkys" for "wires," "tablecloths in Shakey's Pizza Parlors" for "roses," "minty-fresh mouthwashes" for "perfumes," "Muzak" for "music," "Marilyn Monroes" for "goddess," "lanky model or platinum movie idol" for the implied woman in Shakespeare's closing lines "I think my love as rare / As any she belied with false compare." The natural imagery in Shakespeare's poem has been replaced with name-brand products or commercialized phrases and images, highlighting the pervasiveness and primacy of consumerism in Americans' daily lives. These substitutions recall the original in specific ways (e.g., Liquid Paper and snow are both white), encouraging the reader to make the comparison. By substituting commercialized objects for the natural imagery, Mullen suggests that women are commodified. Even though Mullen's poem retains the sense of the original, the closing of each poem sends a very different message. Notably, Mullen's takes on Shakespeare's "Sonnet 130" are formatted as prose poems. In her chapter, "Harryette Mullen's Poetics in Prose: A Return to the Modernist Hybrid" in her book *American Hybrid Poetics: Gender, Mass Culture, and Form*, Amy Moorman Robbins argues that Mullen's prose poems can be read as boxes that "replicate and resist . . . established cultural biases surrounding gender and race" (101). Using this strategy, we can read the prose poem form of Mullen's recastings of "Sonnet 130" as further emphasis on the ways that women are commodified and boxed-in/boxed-up by society.

Shakespeare's poem of false compare critiques the poetic conventions of the blazon that make unrealistic evaluations of women's beauty. There are two major types of blazon: *blason satirique* and *blason medallon*. The purpose of the former is satiric; that of the latter is to describe briefly a single object. Historically, *blason medallon* celebrated some part of the female body ("Blason" 141–42). In a sense, Shakespeare's sonnet blends the two types of blazon since it uses the conventional structure of a *blason medallon* to satirize the genre. In the last line the speaker calls his mistress "as rare" as any woman compared in such hyperbolic terms as can be found in many *blasons medallons*. Though this rarity undoubtedly speaks to the mistress's beauty, it could also speak to nonphysical attributes of the woman, such as her character or intelligence. In Mullen's version the final lines send a different message: "my scrumptious Twinkie has as much sex appeal for me as any lanky model or platinum movie idol who's hyped beyond belief" (*SWTD* 20). Here, the rarity in Shakespeare's poem is translated into "sex appeal," which indicates that the woman in this poem is seen primarily as a sexual object. This idea is further emphasized by the phrase "for me," which shows that the speaker sees the woman as an object that can fulfill their own desires. That Mullen's poem repeatedly compares the woman to commodities and ultimately evaluates her as a sex object is no coincidence. By doing so, Mullen shows the connection between a society's obsession with consumerism and the objectification of women.

The use of humor and experimental poetics to critique American capitalism is not unique to Mullen, of course. Published in 2001, the same year as *Sleeping with the Dictionary*, Charles Bernstein's *With Strings* uses similar strategies as Mullen's book. There is Oulipian procedural play (indeed one poem is titled "O! Li Po!"), frequent critique of capitalism, often generated by humor, and near-constant revelry in the textures and sounds of language. As in "Jingle Jangle," many of Bernstein's poems act as a kind of language recorder or, more accurately in Bernstein's case, a language scrambler, mixing many phrases, such as we see in "ruminative ablution," "What's sauce for the gander / Is gravy for the geese" and narratives we are exposed to in American society (71). There is also a shared affinity for difficulty or challenge. The epigraph of Bernstein's book is a twelfth-century poem by Giraut de Bornelh that serves as an *ars poetica* for Bernstein. The poem describes critics who implore the poet to "sing lighter songs," instead of challenging ones, insisting that doing so would improve the poet's life, but the poet refuses, saying,

> But it's my creed
> That these songs yield
> No value at the commencing
> Only later, when one earns it.

Indeed, we might read this poem as a refiguring of value in a capitalist society. Value, in Bernstein's opinion, should be earned through thought and work, not arbitrarily assigned or ascribed to frivolous, superficial objects. In "log rhythms," Bernstein questions skewed capitalist values that, as we saw in "European Folktale Variant," favor property over human life: "Survival / without dignity that's one thing; but survival / without property?" (122). Later in the same poem, Bernstein laments how, because of capitalism, we have strayed from the ethical concerns of John Stuart Mill, stating, "Capitalism may not / be destiny but it sure feels like it" (123). Indeed, these ethical concerns and their relationship to poetry and capitalism—later in the same poem, there is an extended conversation on hedonistic ethics between the lox and the frown (an obvious play on the fox and the hound) about what constitutes "the good" and whether we should be concerned about what is good for each individual or for people as a whole—seem to be the heart of Bernstein's book.

A key difference between Mullen's and Bernstein's work is the role of identity. Although Mullen resists using a lyric "I" in order to avoid overly reductive readings that limit subjectivity, she foregrounds issues of identity, especially race and gender. As we have seen, Mullen modifies Oulipian techniques, such as substituting chosen words in S + 7 poems instead of random ones, to allow for more authorial input and more direct political critique. One critique of "language"-based poetics is that it eschews opportunities for engaging with identity by focusing on the text. Bernstein, in his "in place of a preface a preface," which begins the collection, writes, "we used to say the artist would drop away and there would just be the work. Can we go further and say the work drops away and in its place there are stations, staging sites, or blank points of radical metamorphosis? Only when we experience this as an emplacement of textuality into material sensory-perceptual fields—turning ever further away from ideality in the pursuit of an ultimate concretion" (xi). Here, Bernstein asks if we can go farther than simply divorcing the author from the text and problematize the autonomy of the text itself. Indeed, in the "Notes and Acknowledgments," Bernstein describes the organizational structure of *With Strings* as "a vortex, with each poem furthering the momentum of the book while curving its arc of attentional energy. The structure is modular: a short work might become part of a serial poem or a section of a serial poem might stand on its own. The effect is to make the book as a whole a string of interchanging parts" (131). This structural principle exemplifies his premise in the preface that the text need not be autonomous. Bernstein claims that in this vortex "political, social, ethical, and textual investigations intermingle, presenting a linguistic echo chamber in which themes, moods, and perceptions are permuted, modulated, reverberated, and further extended" (131). Although this concept presents interesting potential for exploring language and ideas, a linguistic echo chamber seems consciously divorced from the material world. This kind of separation may allow readers an alternative space to consider how language works on and in the material world, but limits the more direct engagement and specific political critique that Mullen's work fosters. This is not to say that one poet's strategies are more successful than those of the other; I only wish to indicate how each poet's techniques enable different kinds of political commentary.

As we have seen, Mullen critiques the negative effects that reification has on gender and race relations, religion, and love. However, Mullen's work does not just hold problems up to the light for all to see. The forms that Mullen invents with her creative constraints and the humor that pervades them can serve as models for marginalized peoples. The playfulness that the creative constraints and the humor engender undermines static structures of thought, revealing them to be pliable, opening up the possibility for change. The poems provide hope for those readers struggling against societal constraints by illuminating the empowered potential existing within them. If a person sees that language is irrepressible, even when under restrictions, then the bars that society, which is, after all, largely constructed by language, places around that person may begin to appear less rigid.

CHAPTER THREE

"But He Aint Never Been Seen!"

The Protean Howard Hughes and Overlapping Capitalist Narratives in Ed Dorn's *Gunslinger*

Mullen's humorous word play and creative constraints in *Sleeping with the Dictionary* reveal how capitalism enables racial and gender discrimination. Ed Dorn's long poem *Gunslinger*—also a challenging text that abounds with capitalism-skewering puns—is attuned to how capitalism dupes people and constantly evolves in order to sustain itself. Dorn's critique is broad, so it is fitting that he engages with a most expansive poetic genre to explore that critique: the epic. The poem follows a gunslinger/metaphysician/demigod and his band of brothers, which includes a talking, pot-smoking horse (sometimes known as Claude Lévi-Strauss), on a meandering and haphazard quest that is eventually abandoned or forgotten, to find and duel Robart, a paragon of capitalism based on Howard Hughes. It draws upon conventions of the epic quest, the Western, comic books, and other genres in order to create a hilarious, heterogeneous, allusive, and unapologetically difficult text. As Marjorie Perloff observes, "each of the four books is devoted to a specific drug: the first to marijuana, the second to LSD, the third and fourth to cocaine" (xiii). The collection of outsiders and the innumerable references to drug culture would lead one to think that Dorn's poem world is either an imagined world counter to that of 1960s and 1970s America or a fantastical facsimile of the counterculture of that time period. But, as Dorn's poem demonstrates, even with outsider status and drug-induced hazes, one cannot escape the capitalist world.

Indeed, Dorn's poem recognizes its involvement in the system of capitalism. Critics such as Robert von Hallberg have noted that Dorn's "poetry is more intelligently political and more sensitive to wide complicity than that of almost any of his contemporaries" (von Hallberg 81).[1] This complicity can be seen in major components of the poem, including the first description we receive of Slinger[2]—the name most commonly ascribed to the gunslinger and the one I will use throughout this chapter—in the opening lines of the poem:

> I met in Mesilla
> The Cautious Gunslinger
> of impeccable personal smoothness
> and slender leather encased hands (3)

The description, especially the phrase "leather encased hands," reads like a catalogue description of a watch or a desk blotter. Dorn's main character, though a demigod and not exclusively of this world, is depicted in the terms of the consumer society in which he finds himself. Additionally, the quest to find and presumably duel Robart (i.e., to kill capitalism) is unsuccessful. The characters do not fail in a contest; they merely get distracted and lose sight of their goal. In their final encounter with Robart, which Slinger sleeps through, they learn via video signal that he is fleeing the country (*Gunslinger* 193–95). However, the poem moves beyond an apathetic representation of the corrupt establishment and the counterculture's failure to effectively change it. The poem's larger-than-life comedy defamiliarizes the familiar, revealing parts of the world once blindly accepted by the masses to be the artificial constructs that they are.

"The Cycle," a lengthy section at the end of Book II that parodies traditional formalist poetry,[3] as it is written in numbered, four-line stanzas, instead of the free verse of the rest of the poem, tells the story of Robart, an alias for Howard Hughes. As several critics have noted, on a fundamental level, "The Cycle" describes an actual trip that Hughes took from Boston to Las Vegas.[4] One line is repeated, which is noteworthy since this type of repetition does not often occur in "The Cycle." The line, "And human hands first mimicked and then mocked," can be read as a description of the exploitation and subjugation of people under the system of capitalism. Those in authority first tried to "mimic" the people ("hands"), specifically, workers, in order to seduce them into the system. The powers that be then "mocked" those people who worked to sustain the system but who derived little from it. Dorn's use of the verb "to mock" suggests the sense, "to deceive or impose upon; to delude, befool; to tantalize, disappoint" (*OED Online*). Dorn, through the repetition of this line, emphasizes how the capitalist system manipulates people into serving it, reducing them to reified "hands" for financial gain.

However, I contend that this line also encapsulates Dorn's strategy for the poem's political critique. Dorn both "mimics and mocks" the system of capitalism in order to expose its flaws, but, more importantly, to show how it generates myths and appropriates cultural narratives to sustain itself. Narratives, such as Christianity, have been used to support and spread capitalism, deliberately blurring the line between capitalist tenets and Christian values to encourage Christians to see a critique of capitalism as a critique of their faith. Dorn mimics capitalism not only "to imitate or copy (a person, action, etc.), esp. for the purposes of ridicule or satire, or to entertain," as the first definition from the *Oxford English Dictionary* states, but also, and more importantly, "to emulate or masquerade as another; to resemble closely, esp. in structure or functionality" (*OED Online*). In the mimetic sense, Dorn's poem mimics or represents the structure and functionality of capitalism in many ways so that the reader who may not have noticed these structures around themselves in daily life may become aware of them and be in a better position to analyze them. The poem's incorporation of many genres and lexicons mimics capitalism's use of diverse narratives to sustain itself. Dorn's representation or mimicry is necessary for him to mock capitalism effectively, since simple ridicule is an ineffective means of political critique. By creating a poem that represents the logic (and illogic) and structures of capitalism, Dorn can effectively jeer at the system by highlighting specific flaws and manipulations that people often cannot recognize.

One example of Dorn's mimicry and mockery of capitalist structures of power is his representation of Robart, a protean character based on Hughes. Dorn interchangeably uses Hughes's name and Robart, among other aliases, as we will see later in this analysis. The Hughes figure is introduced early in the poem during a conversation between I, which is a character's actual name, a literalized representation of Tennyson's famous line, "I am become a name" from his "Ulysses," a poem inspired by an epic poem, and Slinger.[5] After I asks where Slinger is headed, the latter replies that he is going to a hotel in "a city called Boston," "whose second floor has been let / to an inscrutable Texan named Hughes" (*Gunslinger* 6). As Stephen Fredman and Grant Jenkins explain in their extensive notes on *Gunslinger*, "this passage follows a traditional epic pattern in which city and hero are evoked at the outset" (61). However, departing from convention, Slinger casts Hughes as a shadowy antihero whose "soul is in jeopardy." Finding Hughes and dueling him is the telos of Slinger's quest, as he tells I, "there is a longhorn bull half mad / half deity / who awaits an account from me" (*Gunslinger* 7). Describing Hughes as "a longhorn bull half mad / half deity" identifies him as a Texan, since the longhorn is the University of Texas mascot,[6] but it also indicates his godlike status. Dorn's use of fiscally inflected language—"bull" can refer to a bull market, and the "account" due to Hughes can be read as a bank account—suggests that Hughes's higher powers are those of economic control. The "half mad / half deity" longhorn also refers to the Minotaur, a monster who was half man and half bull.[7] Dorn's association of Hughes with a monster who eats people is a not-so-subtle characterization of successful capitalists and, by extension, the system of capitalism itself, as one that preys upon people in order to sustain itself.

The goal of finding and confronting Hughes has been Slinger's personal obsession for some time, as we learn from Lil, a "cabaret" madam with whom Slinger is acquainted. Lil claims that Hughes is "peculiar" about being seen, referencing Hughes's real life, who, due to mental health issues, became increasingly reclusive (*Gunslinger* 10).[8] But his status as an unseen figure illustrates Dorn's conception of capitalism as a system that withholds its motives and perhaps many of its practices from the majority of the population, the middle and lower classes specifically. Many living under the system of capitalism Dorn depicts would agree with Lil that it is "plumb strange the way" capitalists "operate" (*Gunslinger* 10). Hughes's considerable and mysterious powers are evident in Lil's confusion about whether Hughes moved to Las Vegas or "bought Vegas / and moved it" (*Gunslinger* 10). Although the extravagant claim seems silly—that Hughes possesses the power to move a physical location—his position as a successful capitalist does grant him the power to radically alter his society.

The Hughes figure's numerous disguises and aliases spoof Hughes's real-life attempts to disguise himself. The first example of Hughes's use of disguise is described by the Horse. A man who shot at, and missed, the Horse hardened into a statue, which the Horse decided to auction off to the citizens of Universe City (75). After the auction the Horse tells Slinger and Kool Everything, an acid-head character who is part of the troupe,

> There was some figurante
> standin there in a bucket
> with crutchs,
> he was a "Lucky-Strike Green" fan (83)

Hughes—cleverly characterized by Dorn as "Lucky-Strike Green fan," since "green" is a slang term for money—is disguised as a person with crutches and a bucket and becomes panicked when the Horse starts a rumor that the statue is a Hughes disguise. He is so caught up in concealing his identity that he makes an extremely high bid on a Hughes disguise he knows to be fake. By making the outrageous bid, Hughes, already suspicious in his ridiculous getup, confirms that he is not a local, ironically foiling his own attempt to remain covert.

The premium Hughes places on concealing his identity can be partially explained by the danger of being "described" or pinned down by one name or identity. Slinger explains the hazards of being described to I: "it makes you mortal," "you can be sold," "you can be told" to "leave" or "come," you become "a reference," "you might become an institution" mistaken for "defense," "the Machine / will always recognize you," and you could be lost in "a maze / called a *social investigation*" (*Gunslinger* 32–33). However humorous this passage—a lengthy discussion about the importance of naming to a character whose name is a first-person pronoun—as Michael Davidson observes, "to be described is the greatest danger in the Slinger's West" (129). Having a name[9] turns one into a commodity to "be sold" in various ways within the system of capitalism. It reduces your identity to "a reference," which can be manipulated by the powers that be. The words "institution," "defense," and "Machine" seem to refer to the military-industrial complex, which President Eisenhower warned against in his farewell address:

> Now this conjunction of an immense military establishment and a large arms industry is new in the American experience. The total

influence—economic, political, even spiritual—is felt in every city, every Statehouse, every office of the Federal government. We recognize the imperative need for this development. Yet, we must not fail to comprehend its grave implications. Our toil, resources, and livelihood are all involved. So is the very structure of our society.

In the councils of government, we must guard against the acquisition of unwarranted influence, whether sought or unsought, by the military-industrial complex. The potential for the disastrous rise of misplaced power exists and will persist. We must never let the weight of this combination endanger our liberties or democratic processes. ("Farewell Address [delivered 17 January 1961]")

Many antiwar protestors during the Vietnam era claimed that the United States had morphed into a military-industrial complex riddled with the "misplaced power" of Eisenhower's warning. They saw the country as a type of war machine that did not reflect the values of many of its citizens and did imperil certain liberties. Because of these concerns, fear and paranoia about the government's seemingly unchecked power increased, invoked by Dorn through the ominously vague term *"social investigation."* Indeed, the term echoes McCarthyism, when just to be named in an investigation often meant dire consequences for the individual. With such oblique terms came the belief that people, especially those with dissenting views of the government, could be "investigated" and reprimanded for almost anything. The lines "and drop you in it / your name / into it—" are reminiscent of the Vietnam-era draft lotteries where young men were reduced to or "described" by a number representing their birth dates, which was written on a piece of paper, placed in a capsule that was then placed in a jar or drum, and drawn out at random by a government official. By adopting many disguises and aliases, Hughes escapes such treatment "and maintains his spectral authority over the world of ordinary citizens" (Davidson 130).

Hughes's disguises mimic and mock the overlapping, and sometimes conflicting, narratives that capitalism produces and appropriates in order to assert and sustain its dominance in the West. The ridiculousness of the sheer number and the odd juxtapositions of Hughes's many costumes, which correspond to capitalist narratives, humorously reveals the illogical, conflicting beliefs that members of capitalist society often blindly accept, thus upholding the system. A particularly hilarious example of these odd juxtapositions occurs as Robart is among a mass of common people at a train station in the line: "For *He* was decoyed as the cheeze in a burger" (90). The capitalized and italicized (just in case we didn't get the joke) "*He*" is a gesture of deification that suggests the Hughes figure is a Christ figure to boot since Christ is often assigned the capitalized pronoun. This pronoun choice recalls capitalism's appropriation of the narrative of Christianity to "convert" people while suggesting that those on top in capitalist society are idolized. Although the appropriation of Christianity to expand capitalism that can be seen in such concepts as Manifest Destiny is not in itself funny, the blending of a paragon of capitalism with a fast-food topping and Christianty's son of god is simultaneously hilarious and bizarre, creating, if you will, Cheezus Christ. One reason the concept of Manifest Destiny does not leave people rolling in the aisles is that its proponents blend capitalism and Christianity in such a way that people will not notice the incongruity of those ideologies. Dorn, on the other hand, tries to emphasize the incongruity of genuine Christianity and capitalism using humor. As was the case with some of the humor in Hacker's poetry, this humor is described by Elliott Oring's concept of "appropriate incongruity," which he defines as "the perception of an appropriate relationship between categories that would ordinarily be regarded as incongruous" (1). Oring's theory more effectively describes Dorn's humor than the better-known "incongruity-resolution theory." An important difference between Oring's theory and incongruity-resolution theory, as noted in chapter 1, is that "*appropriate incongruity does not suggest that an incongruity is resolved. The incongruity remains, even though points of connection between the incongruous categories are discovered. A measure of appropriateness is recognized between the juxtaposed domains, but incongruity and appropriateness characterize a psychologically valid rather than a logically valid relation" (Oring 2). Oring expands his theory in order to differentiate jokes from similar structures, such as metaphors, which are not usually regarded as funny: "in jokes the engagement of incongruity and the search for its appropriateness is *spurious* rather than *genuine*. That is to say that jokes emerge when some aspect of either the incongruity or its appropriateness (more often the latter) is recognized as illegitimate. It violates logic, the sense of what we know to be true, or the sense of what traditional behaviors or expressions are supposed to do or mean" (5–6). The appropriate incongruity encourages readers to compare the seemingly disparate things. This comparative process, even though it fails in making sense initially, does provide opportunities for making connections between the incongruous terms, but the terms are not reconciled. In the case of Hughes, the cheeze in a burger, and Jesus Christ, one can make the connection that the terms metonymically represent American capitalism, the fast-food industry, and Christianity, respectively. The fast-food industry and Christianity are institutions and/or narratives used to sustain capitalism, although in thinking of Christianity as a faith many people overlook its institutional base. Fast food, a culinary version of Henry Ford's infamous assembly line, fosters the desire for immediate gratification, which both encourages and is encouraged by capitalism. Additionally, the disguise of cheeze in a burger puns on Hughes's status as a paragon of capitalism, or a "Big Cheese," and the word "burgher," which refers to a member of the bourgeoisie. Christianity, through Manifest Destiny and the ethic of hard work that it promotes, has long been used to support and expand capitalism. By combining Christianity and the fast-food industry in the line, Dorn puts them on the same level, in a sense, simultaneously showing the deflated status of contemporary Christianity and the elevated status of fast food in the US. This social leveling hints that capitalism is the great equalizer in treating everything like a product to be sold. This reading implies that fast food, a stand-in for the mass-produced consumer product in general, has become godlike—that people worship and revere it with a devotion usually associated with religious faith. Through the cartoonish image of people worshipping a piece of cheese in a burger, Dorn mocks the illogical and immoral conflation of Christianity and capitalism and reveals that capitalism itself has become America's religion.

Appropriate incongruity can be seen through Dorn's repeated comparison of Hughes to Christ, which emphasizes the mystery surrounding both figures. Dorn describes Hughes as an "unseen symbolic Body Of the shrouding" (90) and the crowd, when referring to Hughes, later declares, "But He aint never bin seen!" (91). Connections between Hughes and Christ have some grounding, in that Hughes was notorious for being a recluse while the Bible reports that Christ's body disappeared from his tomb as he ascended to heaven. Of course, attempts to equate a reclusive millionaire to the purported savior of humankind are far from appropriate and are therefore humorous. However, serious consequences of this kind of mystery can be discovered. Faith in the unseen is a critical aspect of Christianity, but Dorn emphasizes the danger of such blind faith when applied to capitalism. Dorn suggests that such faith in the powers that be sets people up to be taken advantage of. Indeed, the lines following the exclamation, "But he aint never bin seen!" (91), refer to the famous con of the shell game, "You maybe oughta look for a bean / Under at least three shells" (91). This image further illustrates the danger of blind faith in capitalism since "bean" is slang for money and if people must resort to looking for money under shells, the system is conning them.

Perhaps the most ominous, and humorous, of Robart's disguises is the janitor/Janus figure. Upon first glance, though, this costume seems anything but threatening. Playing upon some of Hughes's germ phobias,[10] Dorn describes this guise:

> While he shuffled along with his feet encased
> In Kleenex boxes *He* wobbled astride an industrial broom
>
> The perfect disguise of the casual janitor
> Who came through Janus from the far side. (90)

The image of Hughes "wobbling" with boxes of tissues on his feet to protect him from germs is silly, especially when coupled with the eye-rolling irony of Hughes, a person seriously afraid of germs, as a janitor, an occupation that requires one to be in contact with germs. However, once the connection between "Janus" and "janitor" is made, the ominous quality of the getup becomes apparent. The term "janitor" derives from the Latin *jānua*, meaning door or entrance (*OED Online*). In Roman mythology, Janus was the god of gates, doors, passageways, and beginnings (Grant and Hazel 193). Janitors are caretakers of doors and halls, and in fact, one definition of janitor is "doorkeeper" (*OED Online*). Although Janus was depicted with two heads looking in opposite directions, the image can also be interpreted as a two-faced, or duplicitous, figure, which is how Dorn depicts Hughes. As a janitor, an occupation of low economic reward and low status in capitalist society, Hughes is mimicking the crowd, the workers. This insider position enables him to dupe (mock) the workers more easily once he puts away his broom.

Another hazard revealed by this costume, later described as "the dangerous disguise of Nobody," is that it portrays the myth of hard work guaranteeing success or the myth of the self-made man. Dorn's disguising of Hughes as a worker, or a "Nobody," alludes to the capitalist "bootstraps" myth that hard work can make any person successful (i.e., rich). Far from starting at the bottom, at nineteen years of age, Hughes inherited a fortune from his late father, who founded the successful Hughes Tool Company (Barlett and Steele 53). Dorn debunks the myth that anybody can become a paragon of capitalism if they work hard enough; he shows that the only way Hughes can look unexceptional is by hiding behind a mask, or, in his case, a broom. Without the disguise, Hughes would be exposed as the "wild eyed charioteer," as Dorn describes him at the beginning of "The Cycle," that he is.

His dangerous disguise as "Nobody" also recalls Odysseus in the *Odyssey* tricking the Cyclops Polyphemus.[11] Odysseus tells Polyphemus that his name is "Nobody" so that after he blinds him by gouging his one eye with a spear, Polyphemus can only call out to the other Cyclops, "'Nobody's killing me now by fraud and not by force!'" (223–24). Just as Odysseus did to Polyphemus, Robart and the system of capitalism are killing the masses by deceiving and blinding them from the reality of their station in society.

Later in "The Cycle," in a subsection titled "The Interior Decorator Runs the Scenario of the Winged Car," we are introduced to Rupert, yet another Hughes alias. The Interior Decorator—who is first described as "the decorator of that Interior," a pun on the Secretary of the Interior—is a character who furnished Hughes's laws-of-physics-defying flying train car (98). The Interior Decorator says that he found "a man named Al whose code name is Rupert" in the car when he first entered (100). From descriptions of Rupert, such as his "amber shades," (108) a pair of which Robart also possesses (97), we can quickly discern that Robart, Al, and Rupert are all Hughes. It is particularly funny—and expressive of his intense desire to avoid being described—that Hughes, acting under the assumed name of Al, finds it necessary to have a code name for his alias. Rupert is desperate to be in control of his situation and fears anything that threatens his position of power. Creativity and independent thought are two of the greatest threats in Hughes's estimation, as we see in one of his aliases "Robart," or Rob art, and in a description of the winged car's shades "drawn against / The organ of the Imagination" (101). The imagination jeopardizes Hughes's domination over the common people as it enables people to see the world differently, not as Hughes wishes them to see it; imagination "Distorts the Interior," as the speaker puts it (*Gunslinger* 101). He would much prefer people to be unimaginative so that he can describe them and reduce them to data, something that he can control. Later in "The Cycle" it is said of Rupert, "it's far out how / He cons the present to hustle the futchah / By a simple elimination of the datadata" (108–9). Hughes and others in positions of power, in addition to "describing" people, can maintain their status by manipulating the media and controlling the facts that reach the public. This type of control is one of the many things feared about the development of a military-industrial complex.

As we have seen through Dorn's amusing depictions of Hughes and his many guises, Dorn uses humor to reveal the illogic of capitalist myths and narratives appropriated by capitalism. However, on a larger scale, the heterogeneous language, style, and generic character of Dorn's poem often mimics the difficulty of making sense of such overlapping myths.[12] While the poem incorporates other texts, such as cowboy songs,[13] it invokes and toys with the conventions of multiple genres: the Western since the plot hinges on the Gunslinger's duel with Robart; epic poetry as Dorn plays with Homeric epithets in a narrative of a journey, alternately referring to the horse as "the Bombed Horse," "the Turned On Horse," "the Oblique Horse," "the Plugged In Horse," "the Stoned Horse," "the Odd toed ungulate," to name a few, much sillier than Homer's "swift-footed Achilles" to be sure.[14] Homeric epithets often functioned as mnemonic devices or were used to satisfy meter, but Dorn's epithets seem to function as aliases used to prevent one from being pinned down and named. Formalist poetry, most notably in "The Cycle" when Robart's car is described as "leasèd" and in the cheekily rhymed stanza:

13   This cantankerous crowd was led
     To discover how it bled
     By the apparition of a Cheeze, in bed
     And do you know what they said? (91)

In addition, the poem alludes to many texts including the Bible, "Ode on a Grecian Urn," Shakespeare's sonnets, "The Raven," and songs by the Beatles. It draws upon numerous lexicons, such as language from drug culture, physics, philosophy, mathematics, economics, and slang. The reader has to adapt to the heterogeneity of the text in order to navigate the world of the poem. Creating this difficult text, which mimics the difficulty of deciphering the world of capitalism, aids in Dorn's attempt, in his own words, to do what he declares writers try to do:

> There are some people who have power and a certain kind of means at their disposal who are trying to get the society to think in a certain way, to do a certain set of things, and so forth. I think any responsible writer is never that. No writer is ever trying to get anybody to *do* something; what they're trying to create is a cognizance in the society of itself, to furnish the means—through clarity of language—for a self-appraisal and self-evaluation.[15] (I 109)

In this case the obscurity of the text can lead to a better understanding of culture. To be certain, Dorn's language and imagery are often clear and often cartoonish, such as the image of Hughes as a "cheeze" in a burger, to expose the complicity of societal institutions such as the Christian church in capitalism. But the heterogeneity of the text complicates any seemingly straightforward, dogmatic messages. Telling readers what to think or how to act would replicate the actions of the powers that be. Encouraging readers to think critically about their society and their position in it by presenting them with a challenging text engages their individual imaginations, as they must, adopting the terminology made famous by the Language writers, act as a writer of the text.

Another celebrated epic poem, *Omeros*, by Caribbean-born poet Derek Walcott, shares striking similarities to Dorn's. Like *Gunslinger*, *Omeros* wittily plays with generic conventions in part to espouse social critique. Of Major Plunkett, one of *Omeros*'s characters, Walcott writes "he punned relentlessly" (30), and the same charge can easily be levelled against the author. Walcott's epic, largely written in terza rima, is more international than Dorn's, bouncing from St. Lucia in the Caribbean to Boston, Massachusetts, to Africa, to the American West, to Europe, invoking Greek traditions and blending them with those of the places explored.

Fishermen's nicknames on St. Lucia playfully recall Homeric epithets. Winston James, a fisherman with a drinking problem, is referred to as "*Toujours Sou*" or "Always Soused." Herald Chastenet, a "plaiter of lobster-pots" with a fear of the water, is known as "'*Fourmi Rouge*,' i.e., 'Red Ant'" (127–28). While various Homeric epithets were used in *Gunslinger* to enact the danger of being "described" in that poem and in the capitalist society that Dorn critiques, Walcott's epithets seem to have a slightly different function. The multilingual epithets of the fishermen cleverly highlight the history of colonialism in St. Lucia. At different times the island was under French and British colonial rule and English, French, and patois are spoken on the island.

Walcott's epithets also highlight the importance of naming in history and to the characters. Achille, in particular, learns the importance of names from his father in a hallucinatory trip back to Africa. Although drug-filled hallucinations figure prominently in Dorn's epic, Achille's hallucination is induced by heat stroke. After Afolabe, Achille's father, and Achille cannot recall the name that Afolabe gave to him as a child, Afolabe asks the meaning of the name "Achille." When Achille admits that he does not know the meaning, Afolabe responds, explaining "A name means something. The qualities desired in a son" and "every name is a blessing" (137). The lack of knowledge about his name reflects the lack of knowledge about his roots, a consequence of slavery and colonialism. The epithets of the fishermen, then, though humorous, are a way to rename each other, to give each other a sense of identity in the world. As Aaron C. Eastley notes in an article on Afro-Caribbean identity in *Omeros*, "One of the most significant and persistent challenges facing diasporic individuals is to form functional identities out of the pieces of the past and the possibilities of the present" (70). The fishermen's naming is one way they bridge the past and the present to form their own sense of identity and community. Although their names for each other are not as lofty as those found in Homeric epithets—the examples above focus on being drunk and a fisherman's ironic fear of water—the humor in the fishermen's epithets is evidence of bonding. They are a form of playful teasing that demonstrates affection.

Clever epithets are not reserved for humans, though; Walcott ascribes them to natural elements as well. Lightning is deemed the cyclone's "stilt-walking messenger" who "jiggers the sky / with his forked stride, or he crackles over the troughs / like a split electric wishbone" (52). The rain is termed "Ma Rain," simultaneously recalling the affectionate appellative sometimes ascribed to Caribbean women, including Ma Kilman, the shop owner/obeah woman in *Omeros*, and Ma Rainey, the mother of the blues. The sea swift that guides Achilles on his revelatory journey to his African past is deemed "outrunner of flying fish," "mite of the sky-touching sea," "this engine that shot ahead of each question like an answer," "this frail dancer leaping the breakers," and "this dart of the meridian," to name a few (130). These epithets for nature are not mere wit and window dressing, either. Throughout the poem, Walcott emphasizes the importance and power of nature and the negative effects capitalism and colonialism have had on the environment. The personification present in the epithets of natural elements goes beyond making them more relatable to human readers; it grants them agency and identity, showing them as peers with humans. It emphasizes that humans are part of nature and that they have a responsibility to recognize and respect the environment. This respect is present from the opening lines when Philoctete describes to tourists the process of making canoes. He calls himself and his fellow canoe makers "murderers" for ending the trees' lives (3).

Protean shapeshifting also shows up in *Omeros*. Although the Hughes figure in Dorn's epic dons disguises that represent different aspects of capitalism, the shapeshifting in Walcott's epic links historical figures across cultures. One prime example is the coconut shell the speaker sees in the water at the beginning of Book 7, which was

> nodding in my direction as a swimmer might
> with sun in his irises, or a driftwood log,
>
> or a plaster head, foaming. It changed shapes in the light
> according to each clouding thought. (279)

The "plaster head" refers to Omeros, the Greek name for Homer. Indeed, the narrator thinks of Omeros as he spies the scene and thinks he sees him, but the visage of Omeros blends with that of Seven Seas, a local blind fisherman who claimed to sail around the world: "both of them had the look of men / whose skins are preserved in salt, whose accents were born /from guttural shoal, whose vision was wide as rain" (281). Blending Omeros and Seven Seas into one protean figure links the Greek tradition of the wise, blind, but all-seeing poet with a local blind fisherman. Walcott's blending emphasizes the importance of bridging traditions, not of considering one as superior to another. Walcott sees Greece in St. Lucia and vice versa, just as Seven Seas and Omeros shift from one to the other. The people of St. Lucia, its Achille and its Helen, belong in an epic poem just as the Greek Achilles and Helen do.

Seven Seas/Omeros lead the poet narrator on a journey on St. Lucia to help the poet come to terms with his role as writer and his responsibility to the people of the island. As in *Gunslinger*, the "I" of *Omeros* is complicated by the author. Unlike Dorn's "I," which is the name of a character—one eventually shot, enacting the death of the first-person narrator—the "I" in *Omeros* functions more as a traditional author/narrator, as a representation of Walcott, but Walcott takes time to comment on the efficacy of this representation early in the epic. After introducing one of his characters Major Plunkett, an expat World War II veteran who lives on St. Lucia, and describing his head wound sustained in battle, Walcott breaks the narrative to address the reader directly:

> This wound I have stitched into Plunkett's character.
> He has to be wounded, affliction is one theme
> of this work, this fiction, since every "I" is a
>
> fiction finally. Phantom narrator, resume: (28)

Walcott's "I" interacts with facsimiles of people from his personal life, including his ex-wife and the ghost of his late father, as well as with the invented characters of his epic. The "I" also struggles with issues of writing and of how to write about St. Lucia. In a poem that explores the complexities of identity, it is fitting that the notion of the "I" is troubled and explored. Later, Seven Seas/Omeros claims "there are two journeys / in every odyssey, one on worried water, / the other crouched and motionless, without noise," speaking of the characters' journey in the odyssey as well as the poet's (291). Seven Seas/Omeros then declares "for both, the 'I' is a mast" (291). The "I" holds up the sails to catch the wind and drive the ship and the narrative forward. It grants vision to the lookout to spy land or chart navigation and for the poet to chart the plot. Walcott's "I" must represent the struggles of his characters but stay rooted to his desk, must write the people of St. Lucia while singing in the spirit of literary traditions. For Walcott's "I" to be a proper mast, it must be as much of a protean figure as Seven Seas/Omeros.

The overlapping capitalist narratives in *Gunslinger* reveal the complex forces at work to keep the system in place. In *Omeros* historical narratives overlap in order to reveal connections between people across time and space and to show the effects of colonialism.

Major Plunkett devotes himself to writing a history of St. Lucia as a tribute to the island and to Helen, his former employee and island inhabitant, with whom he is obsessed. In fact, St. Lucia itself was known as "Helen" because the British and French fought over it for so many years. The narrator reads and ruminates on Catherine Weldon's writing and work with Sitting Bull. He connects the plight of Native Americans being pushed off of their land to that of St. Lucians and others who have endured slavery, diaspora, and forced exodus. The narrator claims that people "take their colours / as the trees do from the native soil of their birth, / and once they are moved elsewhere, entire cultures / lose the art of mimicry" (207–8). In place of the trees, "a desert place / widens in the heart" (208). The "desert place" Walcott writes of is embodied in Achille's struggle with his sense of identity and place in the world. It emphasizes the deeply personal and psychological effects of colonialization. Through this internalized desert, though personal for everyone who has endured displacement, Walcott links people together across continents and centuries of colonial rule, not to discount their distinct narratives, but to highlight commonalities and form bonds of respect and understanding. In this passage, Walcott compares the plight of displaced people to nature—in this case, trees—for poetic effect but also to highlight the often disastrous effects imperialism has on the environment.

Though Dorn's epic engages with the negative effects of capitalism more directly, Walcott also critiques the effects of capitalism's effects on people and the environment. Large white cruise ships loom ominously over St. Lucia as tourism threatens to alter the island with hotels sprouting up everywhere, making the island look like so many other tourist destinations. Hector's death—he crashed his passenger van which he recklessly raced from the town to the airport to make more money than he did as a fisherman—portends future casualties to a changed lifestyle built around tourism. Achille laments the lack of fish in his usual fishing spots due to commercial fishing methods and searches out new ones in the hopes of sustaining his work and life through traditional means. Walcott's narrator questions whether he dislikes the change for substantive reasons or because of a writerly tendency to romanticize the poor through a nostalgic lens. Ultimately, the narrator laments the homogenization of the island and caustically describes the ocean as "the gold sea / flat as a credit card" (229). Walcott's wit in the biting comparison—gold here is not simply a color but a reference to a precious metal, and reducing the sea to a credit card seems especially callous in a poem that sings the sea's virtues and power—reveals how opportunistic people view the beauty of the environment as a way to make money.

Neither epic follows its characters into battle. Dorn's characters get distracted from their proposed duel with Robart, and the main conflict between Hector and Achille—literally over Hector's rusty tin but truly over their love of Helen—occurs early in Walcott's poem and is not overly violent. These departures from the traditional epic conflict reflect each author's concerns. Dorn exposes the hypocrisies of American capitalism while Walcott examines the effects of colonialism on both individual and national identity. Both show how playfully engaging with the generic traditions of the epic can yield complex, insightful cultural critique.

To return to Dorn's wit, one passage above all others speaks to the importance of humor in *Gunslinger*'s critique. It is spoken by I after he was brought back to life by being pumped full of Kool Everything's five-gallon gas can full of acid:

Entrapment is this society's
Sole activity, I whispered
and Only laughter,
can blow it to rags (155)

Of these lines Davidson writes, "laughter is the primary agent of Dorn's debunking power, although the humor in the poem is never of the rollicking sort but the more acidic variety that one associates with Swift or Blake" (117). Although I disagree with his assertion that the poem is devoid of "rollicking" humor—I'd characterize the talking barrels and pot-smoking horses, innumerable puns, and frequent "who's-on-first" style of dialogue as rollicking—the majority of Dorn's humor is caustic and can be characterized as rebellious since so much of it is directed at systems of power or people in positions of power. In *Laughter and Ridicule: Towards a Social Critique of Humor*, Michael Billig explains that "rebellious humor mocks the rules and the rulers. If the social world is full of codes that restrict what can be said and done, then delight can be taken in breaking the rules that constrain social actors" (207). He claims, "rebellious humor conveys an image of momentary freedom from the restraints of social convention. It constitutes a brief escape, or, to use the terminology of Peter Berger (1997), a moment of transcendence" (208). In other words, it can aid in combating, if only momentarily, the entrapment of which I speaks. Although it is often directed at the powerful, rebellious humor does not necessarily equal rebellion, as Billig points out: "at times rebellious humour—or humour that is claimed and experienced as rebellious—can have conservative or disciplinary functions. Far from subverting the serious world of power, the humour can strengthen it" (212). One means by which rebellious humor can strengthen authority is by causing self-deception (213). It is all too easy to consider oneself rebellious if one engages in rebellious humor when humor alone may achieve nothing. Dorn's poem does not enable such self-delusion because it encourages, to borrow his words, "self-appraisal and self-evaluation" (*Interviews* 109).

The stylistic double movement of Dorn's mimicking and mocking resonates with Linda Hutcheon's description of postmodern parody:

> Parody—often called ironic quotation, pastiche, appropriation, or intertextuality—is usually considered central to postmodernism, both by its detractors and its defenders. For artists, the postmodern

is said to involve a rummaging through the image reserves of the past in such a way as to show the history of the representations their parody calls to our attention.... But this parodic reprise of the past of art is not nostalgic; it is always critical. It is also not ahistorical or dehistoricizing; it does not wrest past art from its original historical context and reassemble it into some sort of presentist spectacle. Instead, through a double process of installing and ironizing, parody signals how present representations come from past ones and what ideological consequences derive from both continuity and difference. (93)

"Installing and ironizing" is analogous to Dorn's mimicking and mocking. Dorn shows his characters to be complicit with capitalism, which he represents (mimics) to critique (mock) it. Hutcheon's description of postmodern parody also provides insight into Dorn's critique of capitalism:

> parody is doubly coded in political terms: it both legitimizes and subverts that which it parodies. This kind of authorized transgression is what makes it a ready vehicle for the political contradictions of postmodernism at large. Parody can be used as a self-reflexive technique that points to art as art, but also to art as inescapably bound to its aesthetic and even social past. Its ironic reprise also offers an internalized sign of a certain self-consciousness about our culture's means of ideological legitimation. (97)

Although this legitimization may seem counterproductive in a text that critiques dominant cultural ideologies, it actually plays a crucial part in Dorn's critique. The process of legitimization is mimetic. By representing capitalism, Dorn in effect holds up a mirror for his readers to see the workings of the system and the structure of their world, fostering a self-consciousness about their place in and complicity with it. This vantage point is necessary for specific, and potentially more effective, critique. Hutcheon's theory of postmodern parody also fits Dorn's poem well because it, like the poem, recognizes the effect of history on the present and the presence of history in the present and, to the extent that parody and irony involve humor, most importantly, the political efficacy of humor, which some critics have questioned.

Some critics[16] have read *Gunslinger* as a Jamesonian pastiche, which "is, like parody, the imitation of a peculiar or unique, idiosyncratic style, the wearing of a linguistic mask, speech in a dead language. But it is a neutral practice of such mimicry, without any of parody's ulterior motives, amputated of the satiric impulse, devoid of laughter" (Jameson 17). Although Dorn wears seemingly innumerable "linguistic masks" in *Gunslinger*, slipping in and out of the language of Westerns, comic books, phenomenology, astrophysics, etc., Dorn's mimicry and mockery has political bite and is humorous.

Others have seen Larry McCaffery's Avant-Pop as an apt category for *Gunslinger*.[17] In *After Yesterday's Crash: The Avant-Pop Anthology*, McCaffery writes,

> Avant-Pop combines Pop Art's focus on consumer goods and mass media with avant-garde's spirit of subversion and emphasis on radical formal innovation. Avant-Pop shares with Pop Art the crucial recognition that popular culture, rather than traditional sources of high culture—the Bible; myth; the revered classics of art, painting, music and literature—is now what supplies the citizens of postindustrial nations with key images, character and narrative archetypes, metaphors, and points of reference and allusion that help us establish our sense of who we are, what we want and fear, and how we see ourselves and the world. (xvii–xviii)

Although Dorn's poem is certainly formally innovative, it does not privilege popular culture over high culture. Rather, it unapologetically references both, often juxtaposing or combining allusions from both categories, challenging the reader to make sense of it all.

In her introduction to the poem Marjorie Perloff writes,

> Much has been made of the poem's political critique, its indirect but searching attack on the Vietnam War as the very emblem of the "Shortage Industry" created by industrial capitalism. But despite Dorn's glancing references to the Four Corners Power Plant, to the military takeover in Chile or in the business deals effected in Saudi Arabia, Slinger invokes rather than analyzes the debacle of postmodern Capitalism. Indeed, it could be argued that Dorn's pop narrative and campy characterization give rise to what is correspondingly a Pop critique of "the Great Cycle of the Enchanted Wallet" (89), a critique that may strike readers of the late eighties as slightly "sicksties" (139) in its assumption that rebellion against "them" can effect change and that the drug culture is an appropriate (and perhaps necessary) component of that rebellion. (xii–xiii)

Although the indirect engagement with political issues and persistent—and usually funny—drug references could lead readers to dismiss the political critique as shallow or naïve, I think that such readings do a disservice to the subtlety and complexity of Dorn's sociopolitical project. Rather than simply "invoking . . . the debacle of postmodern Capitalism," Dorn confronts readers with an unsettling vision of their world, emphasizes their participation in the creation of its catastrophic state. Returning to the Hughes figure, Dorn's depiction of Robart's many guises and their corresponding cultural narratives represent his analysis of one method postmodern capitalism utilizes to sustain itself. Beyond Dorn's own analysis, the humorous presentation of the protean Hughes coupled with the complex text of "The Cycle" encourages readers to analyze the system themselves in order to avoid being "described."

Beyond serving as a major plot device and a political critique, the danger of being described illuminates some of Dorn's poetic ideals. In "First Annotations," Fredman and Jenkins astutely trace Dorn's depiction of being described to Charles Olson, Dorn's poetic mentor (70). In his essay "Human Universe," Olson expresses concerns about the overly reductive worldview of many people and the writing that results from such narrow outlooks:

> What makes most acts—of living and writing—unsatisfactory, is that the person and/or the writer satisfy themselves that they can only make a form (what they say or do, or a story or a poem, whatever) by selecting from the full content some face of it, or plane, some part. . . . For any of us, at any instant, are juxtaposed to any experience, even an overwhelming single one, on several more planes than the arbitrary and discursive which we inherit can declare.
>
> . . . What it comes to is ourselves, that we do not find ways to hew to experience as it is, in our definition and expression of it, in other words, find ways to stay in the human universe, and not be led to partition reality at any point, in any way. (Olson 55–56)

The inclusiveness and difficulty of Dorn's text indicate that he is not content with isolating one "plane" or "some part" of an idea. The staggering number of juxtaposition and allusions on a single page of the poem resists attempts to classify the poem or elements within it. Olson associates classification with "a stopping," which Dorn effectively avoids. *Gunslinger* is in perpetual motion with a trajectory that is simultaneously linear and nonlinear. Although Slinger is a demigod, and therefore not human, his mission, and Dorn's, seems to revolve around challenging people to "stay in the human universe," to be mindful of the complexities of their society, present in their interactions with others, and reticent to accept easy explanations. Such a society would be in a better position to heed President Eisenhower's advice concerning the military-industrial complex: "Only an alert and knowledgeable citizenry can compel the proper meshing of the huge industrial and military machinery of defense with our peaceful methods and goals so that security and liberty may prosper together" ("Farewell Address [delivered 17 January 1961]").

The level of readerly engagement required by the text is high. A common reader could not be expected to know the numerous allusions to physics, classical literature, mythology, phenomenology, etc. Indeed, there have been attempts to make extensive notes to the poem to help readers understand the allusions, such as Fredman and Jenkins's "First Annotations to Edward Dorn's *Gunslinger*," which runs well over one hundred pages. Michelson, after discussing Charles Olson's concern with cultural consciousness, explains:

> Dorn has the same commitment to cultural consciousness but is more like a village recorder, one with an incisive if irritable anthropologist's eye, tracking the habits of the locals. He's an anthropologist with an attitude, but then it's his village. He's not imposing alien standards, though sedition might be another matter. Neither does he intervene. It's a free country, as they say. But there's a difference between freedom and "freedum." (186)

Dorn is trying to teach readers to read the world or to see it in a new way by showing them, often in unflattering terms, what they really look like. The poem's difficulty mimics the difficulty of "reading" and existing in capitalist society. Although not gentle, Dorn is critical in the hopes that readers will not be easily duped by capitalist paragons dressed up as fast food. Dorn, when speaking of *Abhorrences*, one of his later works, stated "the only poetry that anybody might want to pay attention to is the poetry that exhibits a certain kind of aggression towards the readers" (Richley 71). *Gunslinger* is just this type of poetry, and even fifty years after its publication, we should still be paying attention. Dorn's instruction won't solve the problems of capitalism; changing people's perceptions through humor, however, can help produce a more informed public.

Russell Edson's Bestiary

Humanists in a Posthuman World

Russell Edson's prose poems might not register as poetry upon first glance, especially with his use of paragraph indentation and separation. And, in contrast to the poetry in the previous chapters—Hacker's sonnets that criticize heteronormativity, Mullen's proceduralist poems that highlight links between capitalism and racial and gender discrimination, and Dorn's capitalism-skewering epic—Russell Edson's absurd, surreal prose poems do not seem overtly political. Yet, Edson's prose poems, which read like mutated fables, draw readers into a strange, darkly comic world that reveals the flaws of our own. Edson's poetry does not directly assert cultural critique, but because it explores the subjectivity of nonhumans and questions the way that people narrativize their lives, I argue that it is politically relevant.

"Of the Snake and the Horse," from Russell Edson's 1964 collection *The Very Thing That Happens*, exemplifies his wacky engagement with the genre of fable. Typically, fables are short stories with a moral lesson in which animals or inanimate objects function as the characters. Although often told to children to help them understand ethical values, whether religious or social, Edson's prose poems—for that is the generic label he uses—reveal through their absurdity the potential danger in such seemingly harmless tales to the society in which they are told and to the animate and inanimate inhabitants in the surrounding environment. Although the father and mother in "Of the Snake and the Horse" seem utterly ridiculous for describing the titular animals' existence solely in terms of their relationship to humans—the snake "comes to remind humankind that fear has form and evil shape" and, hilariously, the father claims that "the horse was invented by man after the horseless carriage" was invented—the latent hazard of this anthropocentric worldview is shown in the poem's violence. Beyond viewing the horse as a man-made invention, they see its primary function as a "weapon" to kill the snake. Mother says, "the horse tramples the snake, doesn't it, father, because the horse is on the side of humankind" (23). With macabre humor Edson is grotesquely demonstrating that when people see themselves as the center of the universe, they are quick to destroy that which seems like a threat.

On the title page of *The Very Thing That Happens* is the subheading "Fables and Drawings," indicating that Edson was consciously engaging with the fable genre. Indeed, this subheading was present in his first three volumes. Several critics have analyzed his treatment of fables, and though I will add to this discussion in the chapter, I wish to explore the relationship of Edson's work to another genre related to the fable: the bestiary. In the introduction to their edited volume *Beasts and Birds of the Middle Ages: The Bestiary and Its Legacy*, Willene B. Clark and Meradith T. McMunn define bestiaries as "collections of animal descriptions and lore, both real and fantastic, which are interpreted as spiritual or moral lessons and often provided with illustrations" (1). Bestiaries, like fables, define animals in relationship to humans and their religious values, but in addition to often including illustrations, they are encyclopedic in structure, seeking to categorize and order the wild animal kingdom. The human desire for order and predilection for anthropocentric worldviews are precisely the things that Edson disrupts in his humorous prose poems. For example, in "Of the Snake and the Horse," Edson has included a drawing. Though one would think it might depict a horse or a snake, it is a rendering of a rather confused looking woman with snake-like curls for hair, obviously recalling Medusa. Although the myths vary—Medusa is described as either terribly beautiful or terribly ugly—Medusa, whose name translates to "ruler" or "queen," is a figure of power (Grant and Hazel 146). According to most accounts, if looked upon, she could turn a man to stone. After Perseus killed Medusa, he gave her severed head to Athena, who put the head on her shield for protection (Grant and Hazel 146). Although Edson's "Medusa" seems more perplexed than powerful, she can engender destruction through her limited mindset. In Edson's bestiary, people often take the place of the beasts in funny role reversals, implying that instead of trying to define the world in terms of ourselves, we should turn our attention to our anthropocentric tendencies, examine the effects they have on the world, and realize that fear's "form and evil shape" is not that of a snake, but often that of a human. Importantly, the woman's snake-like hair demonstrates Edson's view that humans do not exist apart from or above animals, but on the same level, and that our existence is bound up with theirs.

In Edson's wild world where humans, objects, and animals talk, epistemology—more specifically rationalism—is criticized, as well as the social norms that stem from such ways of thinking. He frequently critiques the egocentrism that stems from humanism, a philosophical paradigm that emphasizes the primacy of humans. Much of this criticism is communicated through bizarre situations or absurdist humor, which, when coupled with his depictions of the lives of animals and objects, creates a type of posthuman world. This posthuman world is dystopic rather than utopic, mainly because many of the human characters cling to a humanist mindset. Edson's world has evolved, but the people have not, or have refused to change. The result is a world of violence, isolation, and frustration. As Denise Levertov observes in her introduction to *The Very Thing That Happens*, the people "*scream their conversation*" (vi). The poems' frequent violence reveals the perilous consequences of a reliance on humanistic ideals. Although Edson's poems reject fables' simplistic moralizations and bestiaries' depiction of anthropocentrism and order, taken as a whole they do communicate a message or, more precisely, a warning: clinging blindly to humanistic values is wrongheaded and destructive.

Before analyzing Edson's dystopic world, it is helpful to briefly consider the history of the prose poem as a poetic genre. As entire books explore the development of the genre, the history I will provide will not attempt to be comprehensive; instead, it will highlight those aspects of the genre's evolution that are most germane to Edson's iteration of the prose poem. Although some scholars claim that the prose poem's origins can be traced to sources as early as the first century AD (Zawacki 287), many agree that Charles Baudelaire's collection of prose poems, *Paris Spleen*, marked the dawn of the modern prose poem.[1] The British Decadent writers adopted the genre, notably Oscar Wilde's *Poems in Prose*, comprising poems that resemble parables. As Michel Delville notes, "the typical Decadent prose poem combines a colorful, heavily stylized vocabulary with a deceptively simple, self-consciously archaic diction often inspired by the King James Bible" (5). T. S. Eliot disliked this highly aestheticized prose poem and dismissed it in his criticism, and his "fierce condemnation of the formal hybridity of the prose poem did much to discourage other early modernist poets from even trying their hand at the genre" (Delville 6).[2] Although modernist writers did not cease to write prose poems altogether, as evidenced, for instance, by Gertrude Stein's *Tender Buttons*, the prose poem experienced a resurgence in America after World War II, and especially in the 1960s, when Edson and others, including Robert Bly and David Ignatow, began to publish.

The prose poem as a genre is often seen as subversive, as it conforms to the conventions of neither prose nor poetry. Consequently, many critics have noted the genre's potential for political statement. In his article, "Accommodating Commodity: The Prose Poem," Andrew Zawacki analyzes in political terms Baudelaire's idea that a prose poem can be "cut" at any point:

> The only limit a prose poem must obey—by virtue of its nature as a concrete cultural artifact, printed or written on paper and perhaps included in a journal or book—is the law of the margin: a prose poem's continuity is broken, arbitrarily independent of content, only reaching the end of a line of type-set print.
>
> So malleable is the prose poem that Baudelaire's principle of vertebra-removal applies even at the level of the individual moneme: words can be broken if the space on the page does not allow them to be completed in their entirety. Whereas a word is syllabically divided or enjambed in a lyric poem strictly according to the poet's artistic judgment and license, a prose poem is in no way harmed if the constituent words are dismantled. In this respect, the prose poem demonstrates its relationship to the newspaper column, an artifact representing the proletariat, or at any rate not exclusive to the bourgeoisie. The prose poet relinquishes her power to editorial considerations, yet the exchange is not one of loss of power for her, since nothing could be done to the work to harm its integrity. (292)[3]

Relating the prose poem to issues of class is not uncommon, in part due to the common perception of the lyric as elitist. Jonathan Monroe sees the prose poem "as a particularly amenable site for an examination of antagonisms of class and gender generally and the kinds of exclusions that are the preconditions of such antagonisms" (18). He later claims,

> In its self-definitions and self-thematizations, the prose poem rejects literature's (especially poetry's) dream of itself as a pure *other* set apart in sublime isolation, like the idealist/lyrical self, from the more prosaic struggles of everyday life which all too often "go without saying." Because it demonstrates with such force the utopian desire of both literature and society to open itself up to previously excluded forms of discourse and the social groups associated with them, the prose poem offers a unique opportunity for the study of efforts to absorb, in both the ideological and utopian senses of the word, the previously marginalized. (20)

Although other critics do not ascribe such political significance to the genre in an effort to avoid essentialism, almost all of them, such as Steven Monte, concede its "revolutionary potential" (8).

Edson expresses some of his own ideas on the prose poem, several of which relate to the critical arguments about the prose poem discussed above, in his playfully titled essay, written as series of sixteen prose poems, "The Portrait of the Writer as a Fat Man: Some Subjective Ideas or Notions on the Care & Feeding of Prose Poems." Of particular significance is section fourteen, which I will quote in its entirety:

> Then the prose poem: Superficially a prose poem should look somewhat like a page from a child's primer, indented paragraph beginnings, justified margins. In other words the prose poem should not announce that it is a special prose; if it is, the reader will know it. The idea is to get away from obvious ornament, and the obligations implied therein. Let those who play tennis play their tennis.
>
> A good prose poem is a statement that seeks sanity whilst its author teeters on the edge of the abyss. The language will be simple, the images so direct that oftentimes the reader will be torn with recognitions inside himself long before he is conscious of what is happening to him.

> Regular poetry, even when it is quite empty of content, the deep psychic material, can manage with its ornaments of song and shape to be dimensional; which is to say, the ability to define space, which is very necessary to all the arts. Such a regular poem may seem the near "perfect object," albeit a beautiful box with nothing in it. Which is good enough; anything brought out of the abyss is to be honored. But *is* it good enough?! Isn't static predictability just rather boring?
>
> As to the dimensional quality necessary to art, we mean depth, volume, in a word, shape; substance with a texture of parts that define space and durance. In the prose poem this sense of dimension is given by humor. The prose poem that does not have some sense of the funny is flat and uninformed, and has no more life than a shopping list. I don't mean the banal, high-schoolish snickering that one sees so often in so-called prose poems, but the humor of the deep uncomfortable metaphor.
>
> One does not necessarily have to be fat to write prose poems. Some of the best prose poems have been written by Robert Bly and David Ignatow, and they are not fat. (41–42)

Like Zawacki's comparison of the prose poem to a newspaper article, Edson relates it to another source available to the masses: "the child's primer." Like the child's primer, he thinks, the prose poem should be devoid of unnecessary ornamentation. However, while a children's book has simple language and images because of its audience and intent to instruct, Edson's prose poems use simple language and images in order to tap into his audience's shared cultural images. In an effort to avoid the "static predictability" that he deplores, Edson imbues his poems with humor, often a "deep, uncomfortable" one (although, to the delight of this reader, Edson's poems are not devoid of the "high-schoolish snickering" of which he is critical, as we can see in the closing of section fourteen which muses on the relationship between fatness and prose-poem-writing prowess). This humorous dimension allows

Edson to unsettle the reader's more common associations with the language and images he employs, a tactic that, potentially, could shake a reader's worldview at its formative core.

Edson's comparison of a prose poem to a child's primer connects nicely to his engagement with fables. Fables—short, didactic stories, often featuring animals or inanimate objects—like Edson's poems incorporate simple language and images familiar to many in a particular culture. Edson's fables build upon traditions of the prose poem. As was mentioned earlier, Oscar Wilde's prose poems were fashioned after parables, similar to fables except that the characters in parables are more often human, as we can see in his poem "The Artist." It tells the story of an artist consumed with a desire to create an image out of bronze depicting "The Pleasure that abideth for a Moment." The only bronze available is of a previous piece that the artist created, "The Sorrow that endureth for Ever," and placed at "the tomb of the one thing he had loved in life" (*Oscar Wilde: The Major Works* 567). The artist decides to take that piece from the tomb, put it in a furnace, and recast it as "The Pleasure that abideth for a Moment," simultaneously asserting a hedonistic value system that prizes pleasure, beauty, and immediacy and showing the inextricable link between pleasure and pain: sorrow, in this case. Wilde was a precursor to Edson—just as he was a precursor to Hacker's hedonistic worldview as explored in chapter 1—in that his prose poems refused the accepted moral lessons of his time and replaced them with aesthetic values. Edson's absurdist fables extend this tradition by eschewing predictable moral lessons and breaking with the expectations of narrative.

Just as a sense of familiarity is key to fables' teaching and upholding of social or religious values, so too is it essential in the debunking of collective humanist values in Edson's work. One example that illustrates Edson drawing upon the familiar is the poem "The Wounded Breakfast," which invokes "There Was an Old Woman," an example of a common nursery rhyme, a genre closely related to the fable. The text of the Mother Goose nursery rhyme emphasizes the poverty of the woman and her children:

> There was an old woman who lived in a shoe.
> She had so many children, she didn't know what to do;
> She gave them some broth without any bread;
> Then whipped them all soundly and put them to bed.
> (Wright 106)

It has a tidy, predictable narrative structure with everyone going to bed at the end, lending it a sense of closure. Edson's version presents the disturbing image of a large shoe cum mobile home:

> A huge shoe mounts up from the horizon, squealing and grinding forward on small wheels, even as a man sitting to breakfast on his veranda is suddenly engulfed in a great shadow, almost the size of the night... (*The Tunnel* 206; ellipsis original)

The shoe is driven by an old woman who "stands at the helm behind the great tongue curled forward" and is brimming with children who "look from the shoelace holes" (*The Tunnel* 206). But the poem's title and closing lines of the poem, "The man turns to his breakfast again, but sees it's been wounded, the yolk of one of his eggs is bleeding...," have nothing logically to do with the shocking sight of a giant shoe on wheels steered by an old woman, lousy with children (*The Tunnel* 206; ellipsis original). They indicate that the man is more concerned with his breakfast and a broken yolk, an already unrealized embryo, than with the shoe family. Nothing is mentioned about the family's economic situation, and overall the poem comically demonstrates one person's limited, individualistic mindset, one which humanism encourages. The grotesque depiction of the overly crowded shoe "squealing and grinding" on its wheels, struggling to get around, dramatically contrasts with the lone man with plenty of space, eating on his veranda. Oddly, in a move reflecting Edson's surrealist humor, the egg with its "wounded" yolk seems to have been more affected, albeit painfully, by this sight of poverty than the man has been. Although the poem supports such interpretations, there is no direct social critique. Through the absurdity of the imagery and the odd juxtapositions, the poem disturbingly resists easy explanation and categorization. Breaking with narrative expectations, because of Edson's use of the ellipsis the poem does not attain closure. The poem is ultimately not didactic and offers no easy moral lesson, but the world and worldview presented clearly do have connections to our own world of inequity and indifference.

Others have remarked upon Edson's engagement with fables. Delville claims that "Edson's personae usually appear at the mercy of an environment that does violence to human subjectivity" (110). I disagree with this assessment; much of the violence stems from the human characters' stubborn reliance on humanist values and refusal to acknowledge anything that seems out of place or irrational. For example, the human characters react violently to a curious dog who is climbing up the side of a house in "The Neighborhood Dog." The entire neighborhood seems threatened by the climbing dog whose worst offense is leaving a trail of drool on the exterior of the house. A neighbor is unable to articulate the problem, as evidenced by the vague language of the proclamation, "This is a nice neighborhood, that dog is wrong" (*The Tunnel* 139). The dog itself, not its actions, is deemed wrong and it is not clear how its climbing is a neighborhood threat. Indeed, the speculation about the dog's motives seems perfectly harmless, even if they are described using some oddly sexualized language: "Maybe he wants to get his paws on the sill; he may want to hang there and rest; his tongue throbbing from his open mouth" (139). Yet, despite the apparent innocuousness of the climbing dog, the woman's first reaction is to get a hatchet and chop off the dog's paws: "She might want to chop at something; it is, after all, getting close to chopping time . . ."(139). Although the poem portrays the fears people who live in "nice neighborhoods" harbor about those who, in their view, don't belong, it also depicts a world where, in place of teatime, there is "chopping time"; where hatchets can go bad and melt as the woman's does, "It's soft and nasty. It smells dead . . . it bends and runs through her fingers," in a way reminiscent of Salvador Dalí's melting watches; and where dogs possess the climbing skills of Spiderman and leave snail-like trails of drool (139). These strange elements mixed with the quotidian "nice neighborhood" reveal the absurdity of these prevalent fears and lend a sinister or hypocritical character to the neighborhood's apparent niceness. By extension we can read this house and neighborhood with its scheduled violence—"chopping time"—as a social critique of the xenophobia that pervades certain middle-class neighborhoods.

The woman's violent impulse can be explained in part by Lee Upton's reading of the importance of houses in Edson's work. Upton claims Edson has a "preoccupation with social structures as these master human subjects. This thematic preoccupation is most vividly suggested in images of houses, which are associated with expected orders of perception and experience. In particular, the image of the house reveals calcified form and preestablished and dominant structures within human relationships. Edson compares the house to cultural patterns that enable practices of oppressive violence" (104). I would add that in this poem the house demonstrates the "preestablished and dominant structures" of human/animal relationships. The dog is acting in a way unfamiliar to the humans, and the threat to the house is seen as a threat to the neighborhood and the structure of society as they know it, which, due to the characters' inflexible understanding of the world and how it is supposed to work, leads them to act violently.

Later, Delville expands on his interpretation of the fable's significance to Edson's work:

> With the prose poems of Russell Edson, the allegorical value of the parable or fable has definitely ceased to be didactic, or even

ceased to exist altogether, as is the case in many prose poems, which tend to refer to nothing but the literal matter-of-factness of their miniature realms, or even merely to the process of their own composition. One could still object, however, that Edson's poems have retained at least some of the allegorical potential of the older tradition of the parable and the fable: an impulse to illustrate on a microcosmic scale the "universal" anxieties of the common unconscious. (123)

I argue that Edson's poems are not merely self-contained or self-referential and that they do possess a kind of allegorical potential, though not the naïve one, to borrow Northrop Frye's term, that so many traditional fables possess. Returning to "The Neighborhood Dog," we can read the neighborhood suspicion of the dog as representing suspicion toward classes or races who are thought to be out of place in certain locations. Although it is not a simple allegory due to the absurd elements of the poem described above, Edson's poetry can be read as social allegory.

Perhaps the allegorical potential of Edson's poems can best be expressed in his own words. His poem "Allegory" begins, "Humpty Dumpty is a man's head; an allegory about a man cracking up, as it were. Then all the king's horses and all the king's men can't put Humpty Dumpty back together again" (*The Tormented Mirror* 68). The poem then ponders the identity of the horses and men and deduces that "they're psychiatrists" (*The Tormented Mirror* 68). After jumping to discuss Hansel and Gretel who "kill [an old woman] and eat her house," the speaker declares, "Hansel and Gretel are really termites disguised as children" and later asks "do you really think that Little Jack Horner stuck his finger in a pie?" (*The Tormented Mirror* 68). Although hilariously poking fun at literary interpretation and human gullibility on one level, this poem illustrates the potential, and often the point, of Edson's allegory: to show, borrowing the words of the poem, "that nothing is as it seems" (*The Tormented Mirror* 68).

One frequent target of Edson's ridicule is rationalism. As Donald Hardy claims in his essay on Edson's humor,

> Edson's critique of rationalism includes not only spoofs on basic human activities such as eating, but also attacks on all attempts to define the individual human as unique and separate from both the remainder of the animal world, including other humans, and the inanimate world—especially the attempts to do so in science, history, art and philosophy.... Thus, in Edson's world there is more interaction between humans and the animal world than we would normally like to assume. Men marry automobiles, fathers allow their virgin daughters to be courted by airplanes, husbands suspect their wives of having affairs with monkeys which they then have for dinner, cruel farmers are murdered by "hooligan rabbits." (96)

This relentless critique of rationalism coupled with the heightened presence and agency of animals and inanimate objects is what fuels my suggestion that we can gain a better understanding of Edson's oeuvre by considering its relationship to bestiaries.

As was noted in this chapter's introduction, bestiaries are encyclopedic in structure and seek to categorize the animal realm and explain its existence in terms of how it relates to humans. Certain features of Edson's work evoke traits of the genre. His titles are almost exclusively nouns and, when looked at collectively, read as headings for encyclopedia entries as the following examples indicate: "Clouds," "A Machine," "The Road," "The Epic," "Vomit," "The Automobile," "The Autopsy," "Charity," "Pigeons." Of course, Edson's poems do little to explain the items named in the titles. If anything, Edson troubles our understanding of these things, refusing easy explanations.

Edson spoofs the need for classification in "The Way Things Are." He shows that the labels we place upon things are often arbitrary and useless. The poem describes "a man who had too many mustaches": "It began with the one on his upper lip, which he called his normal one. He would say, this is my normal mustache" (*The Tunnel* 200). Then the man would place another mustache over the first one and declare, "this is my abnormal one" (*The Tunnel* 200). The man would continue to place additional mustaches over the others declaring some normal and others abnormal. He then takes off all the mustaches, claiming "they like a rest" and the man's audience tells him that they were under the impression that the first mustache was real (*The Tunnel* 200). The man balks at this sentiment, claiming "all my mustaches are real; it's just that some of them are normal, and some of them are abnormal; it's simply the way things are..." (*The Tunnel* 200). The labels of "normal" and "abnormal" seem to have little or no meaning whatsoever, ridiculing the desire to classify, particularly according to the degrees of social acceptability. The man's repeated assertion "it's simply the way things are" makes him seem foolish for unquestioningly accepting these categories as real and fixed, not artificial and arbitrary. Edson's critique is communicated through the poem's absurdist humor. In *The Absurd in Literature*, Neil Cornwell[4] writes about the factors that contribute to the absurdity in the work of Daniil Kharms, a Russian short fiction writer whom he rightfully compares to Edson:

> The dislocation of natural laws and/or narrative expectations, the exploitation of coincidence, of "Murphy's Law" ("if it can go wrong, it will": ibid., 145) and of aggression, plus a tension, or balance, between plausibility and implausibility: "the logic of the absurd demands... that any event—in order to be funny—should be simultaneously surprising, implausible and plausible" (136). Much, of course, depends upon the balance between plausible and implausible: excessive implausibility may tip the board into nonsense, but there is likely to be a stress on all these in "crazy comedy" as opposed to "realist comedy" (145). (Cornwell 167)

The poem blends the plausible (a false mustache) with the implausible (the sheer number of them as well as his classification system), but it does not devolve into nonsense. Through the absurd humor, it highlights the often senseless practice of classifying or categorizing, particularly around ideas of normalcy.

Bestiaries often include illustrations of the animals, which add to their encyclopedic nature, as these pictures clarify the physical appearance of the animals. In *The Very Thing That Happens*, Edson includes many drawings. As discussed in the beginning of this chapter, the illustration accompanying "Of the Snake and the Horse" depicts a woman with snake-like hair, hinting at the interrelation of humans and animals. Many of the other drawings in the work are not as subtle in their blending of the human, the animal, and the inanimate. The first drawing to appear is of an anthropomorphized house: a basic house structure with a human face.[5] Other such drawings include a collection of pitchers with human faces, a man with wheels for hands and feet, a piece of wood with a human face, a bird-like person, a person with wooden boards for limbs, several wood-block people or dummies, a mermaid, a lion made of fire, a hammer with a human face, and pliers drawn to resemble a fish.[6] While the illustrations in bestiaries document human knowledge about the animals, Edson's illustrations of blended creatures debunk the assumption that the realms of human, animal, and inanimate are separate, and furthermore, that the human occupies a higher position of dominance over the other realms. This leveling of the hierarchy opposes humanist philosophy, much of which has relied upon the premise that humans are dominant over and superior to the animal and the inanimate. Indeed, the prose poem as a (hybrid) genre, which, as discussed earlier, has been identified by critics as possessing revolutionary potential, seems an apt choice for creating a world populated by hybrid creatures.

Arguably the most famous and formative of these humanist philosophies is that of René Descartes. In Part Five of *Discourse on Method*, Descartes contrasts humans with automatons and animals to support his claims that, "I think, therefore I am" (18) and that humans possess a rational soul:

> if there were such machines having the organs and the shape of a monkey or of some other animal that lacked reason, we would have no way of recognizing that they were not entirely of the same nature as these animals; whereas, if there were any such machines that bore a resemblance to our bodies and imitated our actions as far as this is practically feasible, we would always have two very certain means of recognizing that they were not at all, for that reason, true men. The first is that they could never use words or other signs, or put them together as we do in order to declare our thoughts to others. . . . The second means is that, although they might perform tasks very well or perhaps better than any of us, such machines would inevitably fail in other tasks; by this means one would discover that they were acting not through knowledge but only through the disposition of their organs. (31–32)

Descartes then uses these two means to explain how he sees the difference between humans and animals, claiming that animals cannot make their thoughts understood[7] and that "they have no intelligence at all" (33). Edson's drawings and poems show as irrational the rationalism based upon demarcations among the human, the animal, and the inanimate. Indeed, in Edson's work it is not too far a stretch to read animals and inanimate objects as, to use Monroe's terms from his quote above, "the previously marginalized" groups his prose poems seek to include.

One of Edson's most direct critiques of rationalism and Descartes can be found in his slapstick poem "The Philosophers," which begins,

> I think, therefore I am, said a man whose mother quickly hit him on the head, saying, I hit my son on his head, therefore I am.
> No no, you've got it all wrong, cried the man.
> So she hit him on the head again and cried, therefore I am.
> (*The Tunnel* 223)

Hardy rightfully claims, "it is more than simply Cartesian epistemology that is held up to ridicule in 'The Philosophers.' It is the whole question of epistemology as a rational project" (99). To this I would add that Edson is indicating the violence that can result from such philosophy. Although undoubtedly funny—the scene recalls *The Three Stooges*—the mother's violent version of Descartes's claim is not too far removed from the original. Just as Descartes defines rational existence by asserting superiority over animals and machines, so too does the mother define her existence by her ability to assert dominance over her son in the form of hitting. Edson shows that defining oneself at the expense of others is a silly and potentially harmful proposition.

One detrimental effect of humans defining themselves against animals is the development of an egocentric and anthropocentric worldview, which Edson ridicules in the darkly comic "Ape and Coffee." We are presented with a human character who sees himself as the center of the universe. This perspective results in an inability to come to terms with the simplest occurrences, and, eventually, in fear: "Some coffee had gotten on a man's ape. The man said, animal did you get on my coffee? No no, whistled the ape, the coffee got on me" (*The Tunnel* 76). Due to his anthropocentric worldview, the man sees the situation as the ape doing something to his coffee, rather than the man spilling coffee on the ape. The man does not know what the ape is and apparently refuses to try and understand its nature; he does not "look" as the ape requests (*The Tunnel* 76). He addresses the ape as "animal" and can only describe it as not looking human. His point of view is so narrow he cannot even determine that the ape is a living, breathing being and not a liquid:

> I don't care if you are a liquid, you just better stop splashing on things, cried the man.
> Do I look fluid to you? Take a good look, hooted the ape.
> If you don't stop I'll put you in a cup, screamed the man. (*The Tunnel* 76)

Because the man cannot come to terms with the ape's existence, he becomes frustrated and starts threatening and screaming at the ape, in contrast to the ape's whimsical "whistling," "peeping," and "hooting" (*The Tunnel* 76). The result is the man's fear of the ape, even though the ape is the injured—or at least soggy—party: "Stop it, stop it, screamed the man, you are frightening me" (*The Tunnel* 76). Such an anthropocentric worldview results in fear, distrust, or suspicion of anything deemed "other." The sixth section of Edson's "Portrait of the Writer as a Fat Man" advises humans to contextualize their conception of human intelligence in order to prevent such situations:

> The human intelligence sees itself as the only thing different from all things else in the universe; an isolated witness to a seemingly endless cosmological process, ever burgeoning as galaxies and morning glories. Human intelligence recognizing its frail root and utter dependency on the physical universe . . . That out of the vast mindlessness was it born . . . Must look upon its situation as absurd. Intelligence is in the care of mindlessness . . . . (37)

Instead of taking human intelligence so seriously and viewing it as removed from everything else in the universe, creating opportunities for confusion and crisis, Edson suggests that human intelligence is of the universe. The circuitous nature of accepted ways of seeing is absurd, and taking human intelligence so seriously results in equally absurd situations.

Although Descartes argues that rational thought elevates humans to a status above automatons, Edson shows that people who cling blindly to rationalism essentially become automatons. One recurrent motif in Edson's work that illustrates this automatism is that of puppets and masters. In "A Stone is Nobody's," Edson shows how masters become prisoners of their desire to exert dominance: "A man ambushed a stone. Caught it. Made it prisoner. Put it in a dark room and stood guard over it for the rest of his life" (*The Tunnel* 32). The man's mother tries to reason with him that the stone does not know that it is conquered that "a stone is nobody's, not even its own. It is you who are conquered; you are minding the prisoner, which is yourself, because you are afraid to go out" (*The Tunnel* 32). The absurdity of the man wasting his life by holding a stone captive recalls Henri Bergson's theory from "Laughter: An Essay on the Meaning of the Comic" that humor stems from "something mechanical encrusted on the living" (18). Bergson identifies inversion as a comedic trope in which mechanization can be found. He states, "picture to yourself certain characters in a certain situation: if you reverse the situation and invert the roles, you obtain a comic scene" (45). Indeed, the roles of conqueror and conquered, reversed here, add to the comedic nature of the poem. Additionally, the man repeatedly, and rather robotically, asserts that he guards the stone because it is by definition "the captured" since he caught it (*The Tunnel* 32). The absurdity of the situation is heightened because the captive is a stone, not someone or something that would require a guard at all. Bergson sees inversion as a "process that consists in looking upon life as a repeating mechanism, with reversible action and interchangeable parts," counter to life's constant change (48). Through comic inversion Edson shows that asserting superiority over other people, animals or things, often results in the stagnation and mechanization of a life.

Edson uses the masters and puppets trope to critique people's reliance on codified ideologies, such as religion. For Edson, religious ideologies lead to a stifling, hierarchical worldview, similar to the worldview inherent to bestiaries, which is described here: "In Augustine's *De doctrina christiana*, Creation was a mirror of the Creator, a means of revealing his nature and his intentions for life and salvation of the Christian believer. It is this view which informs the bestiary, whose prime function was clearly to present Christian teachings in an easily comprehended, indeed appealing manner to a broad audience" (quoted in Clark and McMunn

5–6). Bestiaries strip the animals of their individuality and use them as mere illustrations for moral lessons. A similarly stifling religious hierarchy can be seen in Edson's "The Marionettes of Distant Masters," in which "A pianist dreams that he's hired by a wrecking company to ruin a piano with his fingers" (*The Tunnel* 147). When it comes time for the "wrecking concert," the pianist sees "a butterfly annoying a flower in his window box. He wonders if the police should be called. Then he thinks maybe the butterfly is just a marionette being manipulated by its master from the window above" (*The Tunnel* 147). More butterflies arrive, and the pianist wonders if they are also controlled by puppet-masters. Religion, or "The Cosmic Plan" is depicted as a series of "Distant Masters" manipulating marionettes creating "a universe webbed with strings" (*The Tunnel* 147). This world is literally one of automatons as both the marionettes and the masters perform mechanical tasks. While the marionettes, a group which includes the pianist since he imagines that the butterflies are themselves masters who are manipulating him, "yearn for a predictability that can stave off anxiety" (Upton 111), recalling the overly reductive nature of bestiaries, God is revealed as a puppet master, and religious followers become puppets or slaves to their religion. Indeed, the pianist inhabits a world in which he ends up unquestioningly in a role where he will destroy what he loves and what he depends upon for his livelihood—the piano—destroying his own miniature universe webbed with strings.

Although religion can turn one into a puppet, Edson also shows how it fosters a sense of godliness, or a tendency to view oneself as the center of the universe, as shown in "The Mountain Climber," which begins with the speaker's hilarious revelation: "It is only after I reach the top of the mountain that I discover that it is not a mountain, that I have been crawling across the floor of my bedroom all of my life . . ." (*The Tunnel* 162). The speaker concludes that he must figure out how to proceed immediately to prevent additional time-wasting. He boldly declares, "This *is* the top of a mountain. How could it be else? . . . The Universe has entrusted me to myself. And I shall not fail that trust . . . I have been chosen to be me—OVER HOW MANY OTHERS?!" (*The Tunnel* 162). The self-deluded self-importance of the character is staggering, amplified by Edson's use of both all-caps and an interrobang, and his musings about his relationship to the Universe recall the idea present in bestiaries—and also in much Romantic lyric poetry—of seeing the Creator through the Creation. The mountain climber takes this idea to the extreme, which results in his grandiose exclamations, "I inherit the Universe! I am the Universe!" (*The Tunnel* 162) The poem puns on the character's bloated sense of self in the last paragraph with his mountaintop meal "served by a helium maître d' balloon on inflated silver dishes," and the mountain climber seems ridiculous as he has trekked nothing but his bedroom floor (*The Tunnel* 162). However, a person, especially someone in a position of power, with such an inflated sense of self and entitlement can engender the destruction or desolation of others and their environs. Indeed, his proclamations smack of the language used to justify Manifest Destiny and the violence used to achieve that plan.

This type of egotistical thought encourages isolation and avoidance, as Edson's wonderfully strange poem "My Head" illustrates:

> This is the street where my head lives, smoking cigarettes. I pass here and see it lying half asleep on a windowsill on my way to school where I study microbiology, which I finally give up because it all seems too small to have very much meaning in a world which I attempt to live in. (*The Tunnel* 208)

After renouncing the study of microbiology, the speaker tries and abandons the study of physics because they find that they "have entered a world even smaller than microbiology" (*The Tunnel* 208). Astronomy is similarly dismissed after the speaker learns that the light they see from stars could have taken billions of years to reach their eyes. The speaker is overly concerned with themself and "the world [they] attempt to live in." Because of this singular focus, the speaker's sense of scale is distorted, and they cannot reconcile the idea of different systems operating on a level that they cannot see or that can render them insignificant. Focusing so much on one's existence and rejecting anything that seems unrelated to it results in alienation from the world. The fact that the speaker's head seems separate from their body—delightfully ironic since the headless, and therefore brainless, body seems to be the one attempting all of the areas of study—emphasizes the detachment between mind and body that an egocentric worldview can create. The human reason represented by the head has alienated the human from itself as a physical, animal being.

As we have seen, in the world of Edson's poems, characters who cling to rationalism and humanism perceive themselves as threatened by anything out of the ordinary and strike out violently when so threatened. They often end up feeling isolated from others, and even, as in the case described in "My Head," disconnected from themselves through a humanist mind/body division taken to the extreme. Edson's bestiary does not communicate an ideology by co-opting the subjectivity of others. Instead, it depicts the limitations and dangers of fully embracing humanist ideology, especially that doing so grants some power at the expense of subjugating others. That Edson's world is one in which humans, animals, and inanimate objects often seem to possess a similar level of intelligence and agency makes it seem initially like a posthumanist world. However, the human characters often cannot or refuse to recognize the subjectivity of animals and inanimate objects, even when their subjectivity seems heightened through their abilities to speak directly to humans or act in ways that one would expect of humans. The humans, as humanists in a posthuman world, are the source of their own frequent feelings of threat and fear, not the talking apes, etc. The world Edson creates in his prose poetry dramatizes how much we rely upon humanist values and ignore other possibilities, doing violence to others' subjectivities in the process.

Scholarship on posthumanism can help illuminate the stakes of Edson's work. In the introduction to *Animal Rites*, Cary Wolfe points out the persistence of humanism in the humanities and social sciences:

> much of what we call cultural studies situates itself squarely, if only implicitly, on what looks to me more and more like a fundamental repression that underlies most ethical and political discourse: repressing the question of nonhuman subjectivity, taking it for granted that the subject is always already human. This means, to put a finer point on it, that debates in the humanities and social sciences between well-intentioned critics of racism, (hetero)sexism, classism, and all other –isms that are the stock-in-trade of cultural studies almost always remain locked within an unexamined framework of *speciesism*. This framework, like its cognates, involves systematic discrimination against an other based solely on a genetic characteristic—in this case, species. In the light of developments in cognitive science, ethology, and other fields over the past twenty years, however, it seems clear that there is no longer any good reason to take it for granted that the theoretical, ethical, and political question of the subject is automatically coterminous with the species *Homo sapiens* and everything else.
>
> That my assertion might seem rather rash or even quaintly lunatic fringe to most scholars and critics in the humanities and social sciences only confirms my contention: most of us remain humanists to the core, even as we claim for our work an epistemological break with humanism itself. (1)

Edson's work, by leveling the playing field and exaggerating the similarities among humans, nonhuman animals, and inanimate objects, shows just how irrational certain aspects of humanism are when we cannot ignore the agency and subjectivity of nonhumans. His world also indicates how stubbornly people cling to humanist ideals, even when their world blatantly reveals them to be false, stifling, or harmful.

Wolfe claims that "the *institution* of speciesism" is "fundamental ... to the formation of Western subjectivity and sociality as such, an institution that relies on the tacit agreement that the full transcendence of the "human" requires the sacrifice of the "animal" and the animalistic" (2).

As we saw in Descartes's work, animals were, in a sense, "sacrificed" in order to elevate the status of human and to help justify the existence of God. Edson's work often highlights and troubles this sacrificial relationship, as we can see in "The Fisherman and the Machine":

> An old man who was fishing caught an ancient machine on the further bank. The old man pulled but the machine decided if gravity allowed it would just stay and pretend no old man fishes.
>
> The old man said, if you're a fish you'll let an old man murder you. (*The Very Thing* 47)

The machine's matter-of-fact reply that any living thing will allow a *Homo sapiens* to "take [it] into slavery, or do with [its] skin or flesh" what they want, illustrates the disturbing nature of the sacrificial relationship between humans and nonhuman animals (*The Very Thing* 47). The use of the word "slavery" in reference to nonhuman animals sounds peculiar, which emphasizes the way humans gloss over such treatment of animals. The man muses, "how can an ancient wife praise an ancient husband without the corpse of something that swims?" (*The Very Thing* 47). The fact that the old man cannot earn praise from his wife without bringing home a dead fish seems silly and pathetic, but it does indicate, in a very literal sense, that animal sacrifice is an integral part of human subjectivity and social relationships. Through the machine's claim that it too is a "child of man," Edson blurs the boundaries between human and nonhuman, which, when taken to the extreme, as Edson often does to absurdity, results in the machine's suggestion that the old man sacrifice himself to please his wife, "If the waiting wife will have nothing else, said the machine, you must wet yourself and go home and die" (*The Very Thing* 47).

Beyond its impact on nonhuman animals, Wolfe indicates that speciesism can have detrimental effects on human animals. He claims that the sacrifice of the animal to elevate the human "makes possible a symbolic economy in which we can engage in what Derrida will call a "noncriminal putting to death" of other *humans* by marking *them* as animal" (2). We can see this symbolic economy at work in contemporary society in the numerous times criminals are described as animals in courtrooms or on the news as justifications for harsh sentencing. But, as Wolfe emphasizes, speciesism has the potential for even more far-reaching consequences, affecting many more than those who break the law:

> The effective power of the discourse of species when applied to social others of whatever sort relies, then, on a prior taking for granted of the *institution* of speciesism—that is, of the ethical acceptability of the systematic "noncriminal putting to death" of animals based solely on their species. And because the discourse of speciesism, once anchored in this material, institutional base, can be used to mark *any* social other, we need to understand that the ethical and philosophical urgency of confronting the institution of speciesism and crafting a posthumanist theory of the subject *has nothing to do with whether you like animals*. We all, human and nonhuman alike, have a stake in the discourse and institution of speciesism. (7)

As Wolfe points out, forms of human subjugation, such as slavery and racism, have often been justified by claiming that those subjugated were somehow not human.

Through its humor, Edson's work suggests that our world will continue to be violent unless we confront our need to elevate the status of our species and intelligence and cease to define ourselves at the expense of others. Because of the extraordinary capabilities of the nonhumans in the world of his prose poems, it is easier to see speciesism at work and recognize the need to combat it. In our own world where interaction between humans and nonhumans is not as direct, we may do well to follow Wolfe's suggestions for conceptualizing posthumanism:

> the only way to think about the ethical relation with the nonhuman other that supposedly comes "before" the social and the epistemological is precisely *through* theory itself. Rather than freezing and reontologizing the difference between reason and its other (all its others), I argue that the other-than-human resides at the very core of the human itself, not as the untouched, ethical antidote to reason but as part of reason itself—the "trace" that inhabits it to use Derrida's term. By thus keeping open the incalculability of the difference between reason/the human and its other/the nonhuman (animal), we may begin to approach the ethical question of nonhuman animals not as the other-than-human but as the *infrahuman*, not as the primitive and pure other we rush to embrace as a way to cure our own existential malaise, but as part of us, *of* us—and nowhere more forcefully than when reason, "theory," reveals "us" to be very different creatures from who we thought "we" were. (17)

Wolfe's contention that nonhuman animals are a part of humans troubles the human/animal dichotomy and establishes a more direct connection between human animals and nonhumans. His concept of the infrahuman both undermines the humanist hierarchy that places humans above all else and encourages a reexamination of human identity.

A final poem from Edson, "A Machine," uses absurdist dialogue to illustrate both human resistance to the idea of the infrahuman and the possibilities for different conceptions of ethical relationships between human and nonhumans that the concept provides. After a man built a machine, he and his father argue about it. The father, focused on the machine's purpose, asks what it does, and the son replies with answers that emphasize its existence and aesthetic appearance, not its usefulness to man, including that it "gets red with rust when it rains," "grows cobwebs between its wheels," and gathers "dew on its wheels," which makes the son "think of tears" (*The Tunnel* 20). The son tries to get the father to engage with the machine and treat it with kindness by "bowing to it" (*The Tunnel* 21). The father's refusal to bow to a machine because he is "human" is an effect of humanistic ideals. Even though the father begins to care about the machine, as evidenced by his supposition, "Perhaps I would soften toward this humble iron work, for even now I feel moved to assure it that there is a God, *yes, even for you, dear patient machine*," he will not show it for fear of disturbing the social order and his place within it claiming, "I would not do such a thing, not with your mother watching, itemizing my betrayals with which to confront me in bed" and worrying that "all the women of the household are watching from the windows" (*The Tunnel* 21). Despite the fact that expressing his feelings for the machine may improve his relationships with humans, as implied by the son's suggestion for the father to "be kind to the women as you are kind to the machine," he refuses (*The Tunnel* 21). The open-minded son seems to believe in the concept of the infrahuman, and by reconceptualizing relationships between the human and nonhuman, he and others like him may indeed "open new doors of history," which the father refuses to do (*The Tunnel* 21).

Another work in a hybrid genre, Anne Carson's *Autobiography of Red*, which carries the subtitle "A Novel in Verse," describes a more hopeful vision of a world in which humans interact with nonhumans. It recounts the tale of Geryon, a red-winged monster, as told by the Greek poet Stesichoros in a lyric poem, of which only fragments survive. Geryon lived on an island and had special red cattle and a small red dog. Herakles kills Geryon and his dog and takes the cattle. Carson presents the fragments followed by playful sections that track Stesichoros's blinding by Helen—he wrote rather disparaging things about her, and she blinded him, later restoring his sight after he wrote a palinode claiming that those initial remarks about her were false. The longest section of the book, "Autobiography of Red: A Romance," is a retelling of Geryon's story as a red-winged monster in modern society. Instead of being killed by a Greek god, Geryon's teenage heart is broken by a bold lover also named Herakles, which is especially painful since Geryon's childhood was a distressing one of isolation from peers and sexual abuse by a domineering older brother.

This modern-day Geryon exemplifies the concept and potential of the infrahuman that Wolfe describes. As a red-winged monster who lives as a human and with other humans, Geryon is a type of hybrid, a kind of infrahuman himself. He is also particularly sensitive to the needs and feelings of other creatures and inanimate objects, usually shown through gently comic interactions, seeing them as infrahumans or as beings with their own agency, internal lives, and rights. Put another way, he is keenly sensitive to things of the earth. Since he was a young boy, Geryon had been working on his autobiography, which began as an art project before he could write and then morphed into photography when a camera found its way to his hands. In the first section of the autobiography, which details some of Geryon's early memories going to school, we see Carson's humorous portrayal of Geryon's delightful sensitivity to earthy objects, such as his feeling for stones after he sees his brother pick one up on the trek to school:

> So many different kinds of stones,
> the sober and the uncanny, lying side by side in the red dirt.
> To stop and imagine the life of each one!

Now they were sailing through the air from a happy human
   arm. (23)

Geryon's ideas about stones sharply contrasts from those of the man in Edson's "A Stone Is Nobody's," where the stone was captive. For Geryon, the stones have "life" and character and occasionally achieve flight. They possess a life that inspires wonder, which Geryon sums up after thinking of the stone being tossed through the air with the funny, admiring declaration, "what a fate" (23). Later, we learn of Geryon's seventh-grade science project about the sounds that colors make: "He lay on his bed listening to the silver light of stars crashing against / the window screen" (84). He seemed surprised when his interview subjects said they didn't hear "the cries of the roses / being burned alive in the noonday sun. *Like horses*, Geryon would say helpfully, / *like horses in war*" (84). Here we see that Geryon's sensitivity to nonhumans has grown more astute. He is aware of the physical states of other beings and can hear life as it is experienced by other species. Indeed, his comparison of roses to "horses in a war" assumes that the people he interviewed for his science project would be sensitive enough to the subjectivity of horses to have thought about what war is like for them.

Instances of Geryon's concern for other creatures abound throughout the work, including musings about captive beluga whales' thoughts (103) and refusal to eat a roasted guinea pig on a trip in the Andes while live guinea pigs crawled around on the floor (139). At one point, humans' discomfort with their close relationship to nonhumans sparks artistic creation for Geryon. After attending a philosophy lecture in Buenos Aires where Geryon is travelling, he chats and eats at a bar with the philosophers:

> It is not widely known,
> The yellowbeard was saying, *that twelve percent of babies in
>   the world are born with tails. Doctors suppress this news.
> They cut off the tail so it won't scare the parents.* (96–97)

Geryon privately wonders how many humans are born with wings. Inspired, after he returns to his hotel, he decides to take a self-portrait:

> It is a black-and-white photograph showing a naked young man in fetal position.
> He has entitled it "No Tail!"
> The fantastic fingerwork of his wings is outspread on the bed like a black lace map of South America. (97)

Geryon's irreverent title and bold display of his nonhuman characteristics makes fun of people's closed-mindedness and speciesism. He combats humanism with beauty in the form of his wings, urging people to accept other forms of the supposedly nonhuman, such as tails.

Throughout the book, Geryon is concerned with the inside/outside dichotomy. While he is attuned to other beings' internal states and ponders them endlessly, he spends much of his time photographing the surface of things. Geryon himself is simultaneously not human and more than human. He sees and respects the life of other things in ways that human refuse to. We learn near the end of the work that Geryon has a connection to "Yazcol Yazcamac" or people who went inside volcanos and returned as red-winged people (128–29). These people are considered wise and called "eyewitnesses" by anthropologists (128). When they return from the volcano "all their weaknesses [are] burned away—and their mortality" (129). Geryon takes a trip to the volcano, flies into it, and returns. After, he is just as sensitive, but more confident in himself as an individual. The last of Geryon's thoughts that Carson shares with the reader emphasizes Geryon's relationship to the earth: "We are amazing beings, / Geryon is thinking. We are neighbors of fire" (146). The "we" directly refers to Geryon, Herakles, and Ancash, who are staring at lava bread being made in holes in the side of a volcano. Yet I think Geryon, himself a nonhuman monster, uses "we" here in an even more inclusive sense than the "we" Wolfe wrote about since it includes inanimate objects as well as nonhuman animals. For Geryon, "we" means things of the world, and he is amazed by all of them, even if they react to him with fear or cause him pain.

These hybrid texts by Edson and Carson contain hybrid creatures that trouble dichotomies—inside/outside, you/me, human/nonhuman—and, through humor, encourage acceptance by revealing our obsession with determining what is strange or "other" to be the strangest thing of all.

Connections and Conclusions

Hacker, Mullen, Dorn, and Edson were selected for this project in large part because of their differences—especially the differences in the poetic genres they employ—in order to show the range of humorous American poetry written between the 1960s and 2001. Yet, in order to communicate their critique, all four poets use the strategy of calling attention to the traditions and constraints of genre through humor. With jokey rhymes and line breaks, Hacker often makes the constraints within which she is working all the more visible, and, additionally, she meta-poetically writes sonnets about the process of writing sonnets. In *Love, Death, and the Changing of the Seasons*, she references her literary predecessors and the traditions of the lyric genre. Drawing upon Oulipian traditions, Mullen produces poems generated by creative constraints, which frequently call attention to their own restrictions by emphasizing and exaggerating humorous aspects of language, such as rhyme or repetition. Through the use of numerous and often ridiculous Homeric epithets—two of the epithets ascribed to the horse, "the odd-toed ungulate" and "the bombed-out horse" are particularly inspired—among other techniques, Dorn humorously highlights the conventions of the epic; in "The Cycle" he also employs metered and rhymed stanzas to do the same for the lyric. Finally, Edson absurdly warps the fable and the bestiary in order to disrupt the overly reductive worldview those genres encourage in another genre-bending form: the prose poem.

In their work, due in part to the poets' self-conscious engagement with the genres, genre constraints and traditions are often mimetic of societal structures or ideals, or of the formative legacy which history has left us. Just as the poets must work within the limitations of their chosen genres, so too must citizens exist within the bounds of social rules and restraints. Each of the writers pushes the limits of the generic constraints, most often using humor to do so, sometimes breaking with them altogether; in their work this in itself—as well as the content of the poems—comes to have social and political implications.

One widely agreed-upon aspect of humor is that it involves a critical distance from the subject matter. In order to manipulate language to crack a joke, one must take a step back and view the subject of the joke from a different perspective in order to express something about it that is surprising or incongruous. This necessary critical distance makes humor a wonderful vehicle for political critique as it encourages people to think about political or social concerns in a different light. Creating and reading humorous political criticism allows people to isolate historical events or structures of power and consider them out of their normal context. This critical distance allows people to see that social conventions and societal structures are not necessarily fixed or unchangeable, even though that is how they are often perceived; though frequently taken for granted or naturalized, these conventions, structures, and laws are human constructs. Humor enables people to see such things as artificial entities that can be altered if they are not just. This is not to say that the poets' humorous engagement with generic conventions represents a call to anarchy or even to revolution; what it more accurately represents is a healthy awareness and interrogation of societal constructs.

In order for society to function, laws and rules are required, but specific regulations and norms should be questioned to determine if they are serving society well or limiting its potential. The poets' use of humor to disrupt, explore, or exaggerate genre conventions mimics and perhaps encourages the process of an active citizen questioning the justness of their society's conventions.

Beyond their shared general strategy of humorously engaging with genre expectations to articulate their sociopolitical critiques, there are some striking commonalities among the poets' choices and treatment of particular genres and generic conventions. Notably, the fable or fairy tale—two closely associated genres—plays an important role in the work of both Edson and Mullen. While Mullen recasts fables, such as "Goldilocks and the Three Bears," to illustrate the prevalence and negative effects of racism and sexism, Edson reworks them to critique speciesism and humanism. Both poets disrupt the readers' expectations for the genre. Edson's poems lack a tidy moral lesson and, often, a sense of closure altogether in order to question reductive thinking. Mullen incorporates language from different, unexpected lexicons into her fables, as when she uses terms most commonly employed in the criminal justice system, to illustrate how certain cultural narratives do not represent the experience of some minority groups. Their similar choice and treatment of genre is apt for the purposes of their critiques since the fable and the fairy tale share the social function of upholding social norms and communicating moral expectations.

Using a technique that closely resembles that used in Mullen's fairy tales and Edson's moral-free fables, Dorn piques readers' narrative expectations of the epic poem's trajectory, only to flout them as the poem progresses. Usually, the epic has a clear telos, and, while it seems as if *Gunslinger* has one at the poem's outset, the poem meanders and explores numerous tangents, and the expected confrontation between Slinger and Hughes never occurs. This aimlessness contributes to Dorn's critique of capitalism, which stresses how the system strips individuals of their humanity and agency. In Dorn's poem the people living under the system of capitalism are lumped together and often referred to as "the masses" or "the crowd." They are passive figures, depicted as blind and dumb—both mute and unintelligent—cogs necessary for capitalism's continued dominance who do nothing to assess or change their situation. Only the outlaw characters or the characters in positions of power, such as the Hughes figure, are developed in detail and drive the action of the poem.

Like the other poets, Hacker craftily plays with generic expectations, most notably the constraints of the traditional lyric. She frequently breaks words at the end of a line with dashes in order to form a rhyme, for example. It is, however, her self-conscious and frequent references to literary history that lead to the most striking moments of disruption. Recalling numerous literary references to the blood from a broken hymen as an indicator of a woman's virginity at the time a marriage is consummated—e.g., *Othello* and "The Rape of the Lock"—she asks her lover: "I broke a glass, got bloodstains on the sheet: / hereafter, must I only write you chaste / connubial poems?" (65). This question is bitingly funny in the context of a lesbian relationship because the importance ascribed to the presence of the hymen stems from patriarchal expectations of women's chastity before marriage, and, at the time the poem was published, lesbian couples did not have the option to get legally married in the United States. These literary references, especially when juxtaposed with Hacker's crude language—"got lucky (got laid)" appears in the same poem quoted above—encourage the reader to think of the patriarchal dimensions of the tradition of the sonnet sequence so that she can expand understandings of the genre and critique legally sanctioned discrimination based on sexual orientation.

Elliott Oring contends that much of the current humor theory is heavily influenced by Freud's notion that humor allows people to express their suppressed sexual impulses and aggression in a way that does not threaten civilization. Although he does not expressly disagree with these modern theories, he asks a most interesting question that encourages an expansion of the views derived from Freud's theories: "Other than sex and aggression, what is repressed or prohibited in contemporary American society that might find its expression in humor?" (72). His answer is "sentiment," which he defines as "feelings of goodness, affection, tenderness, admiration, sympathy, and compassion" (72). He argues that "as sentiments and sentimentality have been criticized and suppressed in modern society, they have had to develop special channels for their expression. Humor is one of those channels" (72). He locates the shift in the perception of sentiment from a positive to a negative evaluation in the modernist era, which viewed sentimentality with disdain (77–78)[1].

The four poets, and many of the poets to whom they are compared, especially Terrance Hayes, Derek Walcott, and Anne Carson, through their humorous political critiques and treatment of generic conventions, seem to share a common purpose. At the very least, their work shares a common vision of the constructive nature of humorous critique. Through the act of humorously critiquing their society, they express a desire for it to improve and—even though their work sometimes lapses into misanthropy—ultimately a concern and even love for their fellow citizens. Although Hacker, Mullen, Dorn, and Edson express anger and aggression through their humor, an expression of sentiment or compassion for others comes through. Their work is not devoid of caring; if anything, it calls for more of it. Through humor Hacker indicates the absurdity of denying people rights because of their sexual orientation; Mullen highlights how capitalism facilitates racist and sexist ideas; Dorn emphasizes capitalism's manipulative appropriation of cultural myths; and Edson's posthumanist critique urges people to see the dangers of egocentrism and to acknowledge the agency of other species. At the heart of their political critiques is a sense of kinship and respect for others. The anger and aggression that comes through in their work stems from frustration in the face of a belief that we humans can do better if we challenge ourselves and express caring and compassion for one another, even—and maybe especially—if we express it through laughter.

Notes

Introduction

1. Of course, not all contemporary American poetry is funny. However, although there are plenty of examples of humor in the work of earlier American poets, in my opinion, humor has become a more prominent feature in contemporary American poetry. The importance of irony to postmodernism is likely a contributing factor in this shift.

2. In her introduction to the edited collection, Rachel Trousdale notes the lack of attention humor in poetry has received and calls for additional research on the subject.

3. Duhamel and Attardo solicited contemporary American poets, not scholars, to write the articles for this issue. I point this out only to emphasize that despite this recent publication on the topic, few scholars have joined the critical conversation on humor in contemporary American poetry. In no way do I consider the critical work of poets inferior to that written by scholars.

4. The completed version of *Gunslinger* was published in 1975, but its individual Books (or sections) were published individually, starting with Book I in 1968.

5. Although incongruity is an essential aspect of humor, there is a category of specific incongruity theories.

Chapter 1: The Good Life: The Politics of Hedonism in Marilyn Hacker's *Love, Death, and the Changing of the Seasons*

1. In "Bloomingdale's I," the speaker is verbally addressing her lover, which is why the entire poem is a quotation.

2. I disagree with Biggs's formulation of Hacker's feminism in the latter article, an issue I attend to later in the essay.

3. An acronym for Lesbian, Gay, Bisexual, Transgender, Queer, and Intersex.

4. See Michael Patrick Gillespie's "Ethics and Aesthetics in *The Picture of Dorian Gray*" in C. George Sandulescu's *Rediscovering Oscar Wilde* for insight into the critical debate of Wilde's aesthetic leanings, especially p. 143 and note 5 on p. 154.

5. Although Wilde wrote poetry, he was a more prolific playwright and prose writer.

6. See Lynn Keller's "Measured Feet 'in Gender Bender Shoes': The Politics of Poetic Form in Marilyn Hacker's *Love, Death, and the Changing of the Seasons*" in *Feminist Measures: Soundings in Poetry and Theory*, edited by Lynn Keller and Cristianne Miller, for an analysis of the poem's differentiation between the rights of heterosexual and homosexual couples.

7. Feminist critics have persuasively argued that Barthes's text is phallocentric. So it seems odd to use Barthes's text in an essay about a feminist writer. Yet just as Hacker rejects claims that choosing to write in received forms goes against feminist principles, so too do I reject that using Barthes's model undermines my argument about Hacker's feminism.

Chapter 2: Bursting at the Seams: Exploding the Confines of Reification with Creative Constraints in Harryette Mullen's *Sleeping with the Dictionary*

1. Oulipo, or Ouvroir de Littérature Potentielle, refers to a group of writers, mathematicians, and other intellectuals formed in 1960 dedicated to researching and inventing literary forms (Motte 1).

2. See Hogue's "Beyond the Frame of Whiteness: Harryette Mullen's Revisionary Border Work."

3. See my discussion of Charles Bernstein's *With Strings* at the end of this chapter for a brief comparison of their poetic strategies.

4. In *S/Z*, Roland Barthes coined the terms "readerly" and "writerly" texts to describe texts that did not challenge the reader to become part of the writing process ("readerly") or texts that did challenge the reader to "write" ("writerly"). Henry Louis Gates Jr. in *The Signifying Monkey* coined the term "speakerly" to describe texts that privilege orality.

5. For a more detailed discussion of Mullen's concern for her audience and inclusivity, see her piece "Imagining the Unimagined Reader: Writing to the Unborn and Including the Excluded."

6. For a nuanced discussion of Mullen's complication of the lyric "I" and her relationship to Language poetics, see Jessica Lewis Luck's article "Entries on a Post-Language Poetics in Harryette Mullen's *Dictionary*."

7. See Elliott Oring's *Engaging Humor* for a thorough discussion of incongruity theories of humor.

8. See Mitchum Huels's "Spun Puns (and Anagrams): Exchange Economies, Subjectivity, and History in Harryette Mullen's *Muse & Drudge*" for an alternative reading of Mullen's anagrams.

9. Stephen Booth does so in his edited version of the *Sonnets* as does Helen Vendler in *The Art of Shakespeare's Sonnets*.

Chapter 3: "But He Aint Never Been Seen!": The Protean Howard Hughes and Overlapping Capitalist Narratives in Ed Dorn's *Gunslinger*

1. See also Thomas Foster's "Kick[ing] the Perpendiculars Outa Right Anglos: Edward Dorn's Multiculturalism." This difficulty mimics the difficulty of "reading" and existing in capitalist society.

2. The gunslinger is also referred to as "The Cautious Gunslinger," as we see in the opening lines, and Zlinger, especially late in the poem. These name variations recall Homeric epithets and emphasize the danger the poem associates with being "described" or pegged into one name or identity, both of which I will explore in detail later in the chapter.

3. In "Inside the Outskirts," Peter Michelson indicates that Dorn uses skaldic verse as a formal model (198).

4. See Davidson's "To Eliminate the Draw" in *Internal Resistances* (134); James K. Elmborg's "A Pageant of its Time" (72); and Stephen Fredman and Grant Jenkins's "First Annotation to Edward Dorn's *Gunslinger*," which notes specifically that on "July 17, 1966, Hughes left L.A. by train for Boston to stay at the Ritz-Carlton Hotel. Later he was to leave Boston for another hotel room in Las Vegas" (61).

5. Until page 32 when Slinger finally asks I his name, "What's your name? / i, I answered," it is easy to read the character I as the first person pronoun representing an unnamed narrator. Early in Book II of the poem the character I dies, a literalized representation of Roland Barthes's conception of the death of the author. Barthes's famous essay "The Death of the Author" was published in English in 1967, one year before the publication of Book I of *Gunslinger* and two years before the publication of Book II. Thanks to Lara Kees for suggesting the Tennyson connection.

6. Fredman and Jenkins also make this observation in their "First Annotations" (62).

7. See also Fredman and Jenkins (62).

8. In their gloss of Lil's characterization of Hughes's desire to remain unseen, Fredman and Jenkins write, "Over the course of his life Hughes suffered two nervous breakdowns," which "led Hughes to seek a life of seclusion" (65).

9. Fredman and Jenkins also note that being described could refer to the power attributed to naming in the Bible and that it "may be related to the Native American and Judaic beliefs in the sacredness of the name. In American Indian philosophy, revealing one's name to another gives that person power over one" (78).

10. Fredman and Jenkins note that "in his later years of mental imbalance Hughes sought out totally germ-free environments. The cornerstone in the creation of such an environment was the paper tissue, 'Kleenex'" (111).

11. Peter Michelson in "Edward Dorn, Inside the Outskirts" reads Dorn's use of "Nobody" as a reference to "Blake's figuration of God as Nobodaddy" (198).

12. Several critics have discussed *Gunslinger*'s heterogeneity, including Brian McHale when comparing *Gunslinger* to Menippean satire.

13. For an argument about the importance of song in *Gunslinger*, see William J. Lockwood's "Art Rising to Clarity: Edward Dorn's Compleat *Slinger*" in *Internal Resistances*.

14. Grant Jenkins also reads the horse's numerous names as "epic epithets" (213) in "*Gunslinger*'s Ethics of Excess."

15. William J. Lockwood also cites this quote in "Art Rising to Clarity" in *Internal Resistances*. He describes the poem's jargon as self-mirroring for the audience, which can lead to self-refection (170, 182–83). Additionally, Peter Michelson in "Edward Dorn: Inside the Outskirts" uses the quote to identify "consciousness" as Dorn's "first principle" (191).

16. See Brian McHale's *The Obligation toward the Difficult Whole* (57), Thomas Foster's "Kick[ing] the Perpendiculars Outa Right Anglos: Edward Dorn's Multiculturalism."

17. See Brian McHale's *The Obligation toward the Difficult Whole* (10–11).

Chapter 4: Russell Edson's Bestiary: Humanists in a Posthuman World

1. See Michel Delville's *The American Prose Poem: Poetic Form and the Boundaries of Genre* and Steven Monte's *Invisible Fences: Prose Poetry as a Genre in French and American Literature*.

2. Eliot, of course, wrote "Hysteria," a prose poem. He was not necessarily opposed to prose poems, but he was not fond of many that were being written at the time.

3. "By 'vertebra-removal,' Zawacki refers to Baudelaire's dedication of his collection of prose poems *The Parisian Prowler* to Arsene Houssaye, the editor of *La Presse* in which he claims of the prose poem, "remove one vertebra, and the two pieces of that tortuous fantasy will reunite without difficulty."

4. He quotes Jerry Palmer's *The Logic of the Absurd* in this passage.

5. Lee Upton reads this drawing as a representation of Edson's characters trapped by cultural constructions in his essay "Structural Politics: The Prose Poetry of Russell Edson" (104).

6. There are several drawings in the book that depict things that do not blend the realms of human, animal, and inanimate, such as images of chairs, houses, and humans, without obvious animal or inanimate characteristics. However, the majority of the images do blend at least two of the realms in some fashion.

7. He specifically states, "nor should we think, as did some of the ancients, that beasts speak, although we do not understand their language, for if that were true, since they have many organs corresponding to our own, they could make themselves as well understood by us as they are by their fellow creatures" (Cress 33).

Coda: Connections and Conclusions

1. Trousdale argues in the introduction to *Humor in Modern American Poetry* that one function of humor in modern poetry is "to promote fellow-feeling and mutual understanding," showing that poets of that time period were not uniformly or wholly averse to sentiment (12).

Works Cited

"Abecedarius." *The New Princeton Encyclopedia of Poetry and Poetics*, edited by Alex Preminger and T. V. F. Brogan. Princeton University Press, 1993.
Attardo, Salvatore. *Humorous Texts: A Semantic and Pragmatic Analysis*. Mouton de Gruyter, 2001.
Attardo, Salvatore. *Linguistic Theories of Humor*. Mouton de Gruyter, 1994.
Augarde, Tony. *Oxford Guide to Word Games*. Oxford University Press, 2003.
Bares, Karel. "On the Anagram and Its Functions." *Zeitschrift Fur Anglistik und Amerikanstik*, vol. 23, no. 2, 1976, pp. 141–52.
Barlett, Don L., and James B. Steele. *HowardHughes: His Life and Madness*. W. W. Norton & Company, Inc., 2004.
Barthes, Roland. *The Pleasure of the Text*, translated by Richard Miller, Hill and Wang, 1975.
Barthes, Roland. *S/Z*, translated by Richard Miller, Hill and Wang, 1974.
Bedient, Calvin. "Solo Mysterioso Blues: An Interview with Harryette Mullen." *Callaloo: A Journal of African American and African Arts and Letters*, vol. 19, no. 3, 1996, pp. 651–69.
Bergson, Henri. *Laughter: An Essay on the Meaning of the Comic*, translated by Cloudesley Brereton and Fred Rothwell, Dover Publications, 2005.
Bernstein, Charles. *With Strings*. University of Chicago Press, 2001.
Bewes, Timothy. *Reification, or the Anxiety of Late Capitalism*. Verso, 2002.
Biggs, Mary. "Bread and Brandy: Food and Drink in the Poetry of Marilyn Hacker." *Tulsa Studies in Women's Literature*, vol. 24 no. 1, 2005, pp. 129–50.
Biggs, Mary. "'Present, Infinitesimal, Infinite': The Political Vision and 'Femin' Poetics of Marilyn Hacker." *Frontiers: A Journal of Women Studies*, vol. 27 no. 1, 2006, pp. 1–20.
Billig, Michael. *Laughter and Ridicule: Towards a Social Critique of Humour*. Sage Publications, 2005.
"Blason." *The New Princeton Encyclopedia of Poetry and Poetics*, edited by Alex Preminger and T.V.F. Brogan. Princeton University Press, 1993.
Britto, Sarah, Tracy Hughes, Kurt Saltzman, and Colin Stroh. "Does 'Special' Mean Young, White and Female? Deconstructing the Meaning of 'Special' in *Law & Order: Special Victims Unit*." *Journal of Criminal Justice and Popular Culture* vol. 14 no. 1, 2007, https://www.albany.edu/scj/jcjpc/vol14is1/britto.pdf.
Carlin, George. *Class Clown*. Little David, 1972.
Carson, Anne. *Autobiography of Red*. Vintage, 1998.

Chamberlin, J. Edward. *Ripe Was the Drowsy Hour: The Age of Oscar Wilde.* Seabury Press, 1977.

Clark, Willene B., and Meradith T. McMunn. *Beasts and Birds of the Middle Ages: The Bestiary and Its Legacy.* University of Pennsylvania Press, 1989.

Cornwell, Neil. *The Absurd in Literature.* Manchester University Press, 2006.

"Daisy." *SpanishDICT.com* 2007. n.d. Web. 10 Nov. 2007.

Davidson, Michael. "To Eliminate the Draw: Narrative and Language in *Slinger*." *Internal Resistances: The Poetry of Edward Dorn*, edited by Donald Wesling, University of California Press, 1985, pp. 113–49.

Dellamora, Richard. "Productive Decadence: 'The Queer Comradeship of Outlawed Thought': Vernon Lee, Max Nordau, and Oscar Wilde." *New Literary History*, vol. 35 no.4, 2004, pp. 529–46.

Delville Michel. *The American Prose Poem: Poetic Form and the Boundaries of Genre.* University Press of Florida, 1998.

Descartes, René. *Discourse on Method and Meditations on First Philosophy.* Translated by Donald A. Cress, Hackett Publishing Company, 1998.

Dorn, Edward. *Gunslinger.* Duke University Press, 1989.

Dorn, Edward. *Interviews*, edited by Donald Allen. Four Seasons Foundation, 1980.

Duhamel, Denise, and Salvatore Attardo, editors. *Humor in Contemporary American Poetry.* Special issue of *Humor: International Journal of Humor Research*, vol. 22, no. 3, 2009.

Eastley, Aaron C. "Lifting 'The Yoke of the Wrong Name': How Walcott Uses Character Names to Negotiate a Positive Afro-Caribbean Diasporic Identity in *Omeros*." *African Diasporas: Ancestors, Migrations and Borders*, edited by Robert Cancel and Woodhull Winifred, Africa World, 2008, pp. 70–79.

Edson, Russell. "Portrait of the Writer as a Fat Man: Some Subjective Ideas or Notions on the Care and Feeding of Prose Poems." *A Field Guide to Contemporary Poetry and Poetics*, edited by Stuart Friebert, David Walker, and David Young, Oberlin College Press, 1997, 35–43.

Edson, Russell. *The Tormented Mirror.* University of Pittsburgh Press, 2001.

Edson, Russell. *The Tunnel: Selected Poems.* Oberlin College Press, 1994.

Edson, Russell. *The Very Thing That Happens.* New Directions Books, 1964.

Eisenhower, Dwight D. "Farewell Address [delivered 17 January 1961]" *American Rhetoric*, Feb. 2020, https://www.americanrhetoric.com/speeches/dwightdeisenhowerfarewell.html

Elmborg, James K. *"A Pageant of Its Time": Edward Dorn's "Slinger" and the Sixties.* Peter Lang Publishing, 1998.

Epicurus. *The Epicurus Reader*, translated and edited by Brad Inwood and L. P. Gearson, Hackett, 1994.

"Fag hag." *The Oxford Dictionary of Modern Slang*, edited by John Ayto and John Simpson, Oxford University Press, 1993.

Feldman, Fred. *Pleasure and the Good Life: Concerning the Nature, Varieties, and Plausibility of Hedonism.* Oxford University Press, 2004.

Foster, Thomas. "Kick[ing] the Perpendiculars Outa Right Anglos: Edward Dorn's Multiculturalism." *Contemporary Literature*, vol. 38, no. 1, 1997, pp. 78–105.

Fredman, Stephen, and Grant Jenkins. "First Annotations to Edward Dorn's *Gunslinger*." *Sagatrieb*, vol. 15, no. 3, 1996, pp. 57–176.

Freud, Sigmund. *Jokes and Their Relation to the Unconscious*, translated by James Strachey, Norton, 1989.

Frost, Elisabeth, A. "An Interview with Harryette Mullen." *Contemporary Literature*, vol. 41, no. 1, 2000, pp. 397–421.

Frost, Elisabeth A. "Signifyin(g) on Stein: The Revisionist Poetics of Harryette Mullen and Leslie Scalapino." *Postmodern Culture: An Electronic Journal of Interdisciplinary Criticism*, vol. 5, no. 3, 1995. *MLA International Bibliography*, http://link.galegroup.com/apps/doc/N2811229154/MLA?u=cuny_centraloff&sid=MLA&xid=3ee433e3.

Gates, Henry Louis, Jr. *The Signifying Monkey: A Theory of African American Literary Criticism*. Oxford University Press, 1988.

Gilbert, Alan. *Another Future: Poetry and Art in a Postmodern Twilight*. Wesleyan University Press, 2006.

Gillespie, Michael Patrick. "Ethics and Aesthetics in *The Picture of Dorian Gray*." *Rediscovering Oscar Wilde*, edited by G.George Sandulescu, Colin Smythe, 1994, pp. 137–55.

Grant, Michael, and John Hazel. *Who's Who in Classical Mythology*. Routledge, 2002.

Gruss, Susan. *The Pleasure of the Feminist Text: Reading Michele Roberts and Angela Carter*. Rodopi, 2009.

Gwynn, R. S. *The Drive In*. University of Missouri Press, 1986.

Hacker, Marilyn. *Love, Death, and the Changing of the Seasons*. Norton, 1995.

Hacker, Marilyn. "Meditating Formally." *New Expansive Poetry: Theory, Criticism, History*, edited by R. S. Gwynn, Story Line Press, 1999, p. 177.

Hamby, Barbara, and David Kirby, editors. *Seriously Funny: Poems about Love, Death, Religion, Art, Politics, Sex, and Everything Else*. University of Georgia Press, 2010.

Hammond, Karla. "An Interview with Marilyn Hacker." *Frontiers*, vol. 5, no. 3, 1980, pp. 22–27.

Hardy, Donald E. "Russell Edson's Humor: Absurdity in a Surreal World." *Studies in American Humor*, vol. 6, 1988, pp. 93–100. *MLA International Bibliography*, http://link.galegroup.com/apps/doc/N2811691937/MLA?u=cuny_centraloff&sid=MLA&xid=0b405e43.

Hayes, Terrance. *Hip Logic*. Penguin, 2002.

Hayes, Terrance. Interview with Charles Henry Rowell. "'The Poet in the Enchanted Shoe Factory': An Interview with Terrance Hayes." *Callaloo: A Journal of African Diaspora Arts and Letters*, vol. 27, no. 4, 2004, p. 1067. http://link.galegroup.com/apps/doc/N2812008914/MLA?u=cuny_centraloff&sid=MLA&xid=15db1e78.

Hogue, Cynthia. "Beyond the Frame of Whiteness: Harryette Mullen's Revisionary Border Work." *We Who Love to Be Astonished*, Edited by Laura Hinton and Cynthia Hogue. Tuscaloosa and London: University of Alabama Press, 2002.

Homer. *The Odyssey*. Translated by Robert Fagels. New York: Penguin, 1999.

Howitt, Dennis, and Kwame Owusu-Bempah. "Race and Ethnicity and Popular Humor." *Beyond a Joke: The Limits of Humour*, edited by Sharon Lockyer and Michael Pickering, Palgrave Macmillan, 2005.

Huehls, Mitchum. "Spun Puns (and Anagrams): Exchange Economies, Subjectivity, and History in Harryette Mullen's *Muse & Drudge*." *Contemporary Literature*, vol. 44, no. 1, 2003, pp. 19–46.

Hutcheon, Linda. *The Politics of Postmodernism*. Routledge, 1989.

Jackson, Virginia. "Who Reads Poetry?" *PMLA*, vol. 123, no. 2, 2008, pp. 181–87.

Jameson, Fredric. *Postmodernism: The Cultural Logic of Late Capitalism*. Duke University Press, 1991.

"Janitor." *OED Online*. June 2021. Oxford University Press. https://www.oed.com/view/Entry/100738. Accessed 11 July 2021.

Jenkins, Grant. "*Gunslinger*'s Ethics of Excess: Subjectivity, Community, and the Politics of the Could Be." *Sagatrieb*, vol. 15, no. 3, 1996, pp. 207–42.

Jenkins, Ron. *Subversive Laughter: The Liberating Power of Comedy*. The Free Press, 1994.

"Jew canoe." *Dictionary of Slang and Unconventional English*, edited by Tom Dalzell and Terry Victor, Routledge, 2015.

"Jig rig." *Urban Dictionary*, 2004, https://www.urbandictionary.com/define.php?term=jig%20rig.

Keller, Lynn. "Measured Feet in 'Gender-Bender Shoes': The Politics of Poetic Form in Marilyn Hacker's *Love, Death, and the Changing of the Seasons*." *Feminist Measures: Soundings in Poetry and Theory*, edited by Lynn Keller and Cristanne Miller, University of Michigan Press, 1994, pp. 260–86.

Levertov, Denise. "Introduction." *The Very Thing That Happens*, by Russell Edson, New Directions Books, 1964, pp. v–vi.

Linder, Douglas O. "Testimony of Oscar Wilde." Famous Trials. Accessed 12 July 2021. https://www.famous-trials.com/wilde/342-wildetestimony.

Lockwood, William J. "Art Rising to Clarity: Edward Dorn's Compleat *Slinger*." *Internal Resistances: The Poetry of Edward Dorn*, edited by Donald Wesling, University of California Press, 1985, pp. 150–207.

Luck, Jessica Lewis. "Entries on a Post-Language Poetics in Harryette Mullen's *Dictionary*." *Contemporary Literature*, vol. 49 no. 1, Fall 2008, pp. 357–83.

Lukacs, Georg. *History and Class Consciousness; Studies in Marxist Dialectics*, translated by Rodney Livingstone, MIT Press, 1971.

Marcuse, Herbert. *Eros and Civilization: A Philosophical Inquiry into Freud*. Beacon Press, 1974.

"Margarita." *OED Online*, Oxford University Press, June 2021, www.oed.com/view/Entry/114021. Accessed 26 June 2021.

Works Cited

McCaffery, Larry. *After Yesterday's Crash: The Avant-Pop Anthology.* Penguin, 1997.
McHale, Brian. *The Obligation Toward the Difficult Whole: Postmodernist Long Poems.* University of Alabama Press, 2004.
McRae, Calista. *Lyric as Comedy: The Poetics of Abjection in Postwar America.* Cornell University Press, 2020. https://libro.eb20.net/Reader/rdr.aspx?b=210001331.
Metres, Philip. *Behind the Lines: War Resistance Poetry on the American Homefront since 1941.* University of Iowa Press, 2007.
Michelson, Bruce. *Literary Wit.* University of Massachusetts Press, 2000.
Michelson, Peter. "Edward Dorn, Inside the Outskirts." *Sagatrieb*, vol. 15, no. 3, 1996, pp. 177–206.
Miklitsch, Robert. "Difference: Roland Barthes's *Pleasure of the Text, Text of Pleasure.*" *boundary 2*, vol. 12, no. 1, 1983, pp. 101–14.
Moorman Robbins, Amy. *American Hybrid Poetics: Gender, Mass Culture, and Form.* Rutgers University Press, 2014.
Monroe, Jonathan. *A Poverty of Objects: The Prose Poem and the Politics of Genre.* Cornell University Press, 1987.
Monte, Steven. *Invisible Fences: Prose Poetry as a Genre in French and American Literature.* University of Nebraska Press, 2000.
Motte, Warren F., Jr., editor and translator. *Oulipo: A Primer of Potential Literature.* University of Nebraska Press, 1986.
Mullen, Harryette. "Imagining the Unimagined Reader: Writing to the Unborn and Including the Excluded." *boundary 2*, vol. 26, no 1., 1999, pp. 198–203.
Mullen, Harryette. "'A Silence Between Us Like Language': The Untranslatability of Experience in Sandra Cisneros's *Woman Hollering Creek.*" *MELUS*, vol. 21, no. 2, pp. 3–20.
Mullen, Harryette. *Muse & Drudge.* Singing Horse Press, 1995.
Mullen, Harryette. *Sleeping with the Dictionary.* University of California Press, 2002.
Nemerov, Howard. *Reflexions on Poetry and Poetics.* Rutgers University Press, 1972.
Nielsen, Aldon Lynn. *Black Chant: Languages of African American Postmodernism.* Cambridge University Press, 1997.
"Nig nog." *The Oxford Dictionary of Modern Slang.* Edited by John Ayto and John Simpson. Oxford University Press, 1993.
Olson, Charles. *Selected Writings*, edited by Robert Creeley, New Directions Books, 1967.
Oring, Elliott. *Engaging Humor.* University of Illinois Press, 2003.
Pater, Walter. *The Renaissance.* Cosimo, 2005.
Perloff, Marjorie. "Introduction." *Gunslinger*, by Edward Dorn, Duke University Press, 1989, pp. v–xviii.
Queneau, Raymond. "Potential Literature." *Oulipo: A Primer of Potential Literature*, edited by Warren F. Motte Jr., University of Nebraska Press, 1986, pp. 26–33.
Redfern, Walter. *Puns.* Blackwell, 1985.

Richley, Joseph, editor. *Ed Dorn Live: Lectures, Interviews, and Outtakes*. University of Michigan Press, 2007.
Sadoff, Ira. "Neo-Formalism: A Dangerous Nostalgia." *The American Poetry Review* 19, no. 1 (1990): 7–13. Accessed 12 July 2021. http://www.jstor.org/stable/27779971.
Shakespeare, William. "Sonnet 130." *The Riverside Shakespeare*, edited by G. Blakemore Evans, Houghton Mifflin, 1997, p. 1773.
Shakespeare, William. *Shakespeare's Sonnets*, edited by Stephen Booth, Yale University Press, 1977.
Spahr, Juliana. *Everybody's Autonomy*. University of Alabama Press, 2001.
Tennyson, Alfred Tennyson. "Ulysses." *Poetry Foundation*, 2021, https://www.poetryfoundation.org/poems/45392/ulysses. Accessed 16 July 2021.
Trousdale, Rachel, editor. *Humor in Modern American Poetry*. Bloomsbury, 2018.
Upton, Lee. "Structural Politics: The Prose Poetry of Russell Edson." *South Atlantic Review*, vol. 58, no. 4, 1993, pp. 101–15. *MLA International Bibliography*, http://link.galegroup.com/apps/doc/N2812063695/MLA?u=cuny_centraloff&sid=MLA&xid=00fe732e.
Vendler, Helen. *The Art of Shakespeare's Sonnets*. Harvard University Press, 1997.
Von Hallberg, Robert. "This Marvellous Accidentalism." *Internal Resistances: The Poetry of Edward Dorn*, edited by Donald Wesling, University of California Press, 1985, pp. 45–86.
Walcott, Derek. *Omeros*. Farrar, Straus and Giroux, 1992.
Wallace, Ronald. *God Be with the Clown: Humor in American Poetry*. University of Missouri Press, 1984.
Warner, Marina. *From the Beast to the Blonde: On Fairy Tales and Their Tellers*. Vintage, 1995.
Webb, Charles Harper, editor. *Stand Up Poetry: An Expanded Anthology*. University of Iowa Press, 2002.
Wilde, Oscar. *Epigrams*. The Peter Pauper Press, 1970.
Wilde, Oscar. *Oscar Wilde: The Major Works*, edited by Isobel Murray, Oxford University Press, 2008.
Wilde, Oscar. *The Picture of Dorian Gray*, Lerner Publishing Group, 1997. Accessed 12 July 2021. ProQuest Ebook Central.
Wolfe, Cary. *Animal Rites: American Culture, the Discourse of Species, and Posthumanist Theory*. University of Chicago Press, 2003.
Wright, Blanche Fisher. *The Original Mother Goose*. Running Press, 1992.
Wright, Richard. *Native Son*. Perennial Classics, 1998.
Zawacki, Andrew. "Accommodating Commodity: The Prose Poems." *Antioch Review*, vol. 58, no. 3, 2000, pp. 286–304. *MLA International Bibliography*, http://link.galegroup.com/apps/doc/N2811886273/MLA?u=cuny_centraloff&sid=MLA&xid=bc4325b1.
Žižek, Slavoj. "Multiculturalism, or the Cultural Logic of Multinational Capitalism." *New Left Review*, vol. 225, September–October, 1997, pp. 28–51.

Index

abecedarian poetry, 15, 52, 58
Abhorrences (Dorn), 104
Absurd in Literature, The (Cornwell), 118
"Accommodating Commodity: The Prose Poem" (Zawacki), 109
Aesthetic Movement, 21, 25
After Yesterday's Crash: The Avant-Pop Anthology (McCaffery), 101
"Allegory" (Edson), 116
Allen, Woody, 7
American Hybrid Poetics: Gender, Mass Culture, and Form (Robbins), 74
"Among Philistines" (Gwynn), 35–36; Delilah, 35–36; ending, 36; language used in, 36; Samson, 35–36
anagrams, 15, 46, 58–62; history of, 59–60, 63; of names, 59–60; reason for using, 59
Animal Rites (Wolfe), 127
anthropocentrism, 17, 106–7
Aristippus, 23
"Artist, The" (Wilde), 112
Athena, 107
atomic energy, 5
Attardo, Salvatore, 4, 5, 143n3
Autobiography of Red: A Novel in Verse (Carson), 17, 131–35; "Autobiography of Red: A Romance," 132–34; Geryon, 132–35; Herikles, 132; Stesichoros, 132
Avant-Pop, 101

Bares, Karel, 59–60
Barr, Roseanne, 7
Barthes, Roland, 31–33, 144n7 (chap. 1), 144n4 (chap. 2), 145n5
"bathtub effect," 53–54
Baudelaire, Charles, 108–9, 146n3
Beasts and Birds of the Middle Ages: The Bestiary and Its Legacy (Clark and McMunn), 106
Beatles, 92
Bedient, Calvin, 60
Behind the Lines (Metres), 6, 10–11
Berger, Peter, 99
Bergson, Henri, 3, 13, 123
Bernstein, Charles, 12, 15, 75–76
bestiaries, 106–7, 117, 124, 138; anthropocentrism in, 108, 125; definition of, 106–7; illustrations in, 119
Bewes, Timothy, 47–48, 63
Bibby, Michael, 10
Biggs, Mary, 20, 28–29, 143n2
Billig, Michael, 99
Black Arts movement, 10, 49–50
Black Liberation movement, 10
Blake, William, 31, 99
blazon, 72–74; *blason medallion*, 74; *blason satirique*, 74; women portrayed in, 73–74
Bly, Robert, 109
"Bread and Brandy: Food and Drink in the Poetry of Marilyn Hacker" (Biggs), 20

Bruce, Lenny, 7
Bukowski, Charles, 7

Cabbalists, 59, 63
capitalism: "bootstrap" myth, 89; Christianity and, 87–88; definition of, 81–82; disillusionment with, 5; in *Gunslinger*, 16, 79–104, 139–41; narratives supporting, 81, 91; in *Omeros*, 98; reification and, 15; in *Sleeping with the Dictionary*, 15, 45, 47, 59, 62–63, 73, 75, 79, 141; social leveling and, 88; in *With Strings*, 75–76
Carlin, George, 7
Carson, Anne, 12, 17, 131–35, 141
censorship, Supreme Court cases on, 7
Chamberlain, J. Edward, 26
Cho, Margaret, 7
Cisneros, Sandra, 50
civil rights movements, 5–6; LGBTQI community, 6; racial minorities, 5–6, 10; women's rights, 5, 10
Clark, Willene B., 106, 123
comic inversion, 123
Cornwell, Neil, 118
criminal reports, 66–67, 69–70
crossword puzzles, 46; cryptic, 46–47
cryptography, 50, 72

Dalí, Salvador, 115
Davidson, Michael, 84, 98–99
de Bornelh, Giraut, 75–76
de France, Marie, 34
de Pisan, Christine, 34
"Death of the Author, The" (Barthes), 145n5
decadence, 26
Decadent Movement, 21, 25–26, 108
Dellamora, Richard, 26, 39
Delville, Michel, 108, 114–16
Derrida, Jacques, 129
Descartes, René, 119–22, 128

Discourse on Method (Descartes), 119–20
Disney, Walt, 73
Dorn, Edward, 11–13, 16, 79–91, 98–104, 137–38, 141. *See also individual works*
Douglas, Alfred, 24
Drive-In, The (Gwynn), 14–15, 35; "Among Philistines," 35–36
Duhamel, Denise, 4, 5, 7, 11, 143n3

Eastley, Aaron C., 93–94
Edson, Russell, 11–13, 16–17, 105–31, 133, 135, 137–39, 141; allegory, use of, 116; classification as a theme, 117–18, 141–42; humor, 117; on religion, 123–24; ridicule of rationalism, 117, 120–22, 126. *See also individual works*
Eisenhower, Dwight D., 84–85, 103
Eliot, T. S., 108, 146n2
epic poetry, 9, 11, 13, 16, 79, 91
Epicurus, 40–42
epigrams, 24–25, 26, 31; compression of, 27; disruptive nature of, 26–27; literary, 26
epistolary, 20
etymology, 61

fables, 16–17, 105–35, 138, 139; moralizations in, 108
fairy tales, 66–71, 139
Feldman, Fred, 22–23, 39–40
"First Annotations to Edward Dorn's *Gunslinger*" (Fredman and Jenkins), 102, 104
Forche, Carolyn, 10
Ford, Henry, 87
Formal Feeling Comes: Poems in Form by Contemporary Women, A (Finch), 33
Fredman, Stephen, 82, 102, 104, 145nn8–10

Freud, Sigmund, 3, 13, 140–41
From the Beast to the Blonde (Warner), 68–69
Frost, Elisabeth, 49
Frye, Northrop, 116

Gates, Henry Louis, Jr., 144n4
GI Resistance poetry, 10–11
Gilbert, Alan, 56
Gillespie, Patrick, 25
Ginsberg, Allen, 5
God Be with the Clown (Wallace), 4
Goldberg, Whoopi, 7
"Goldilocks and the Three Bears," 66–68, 70, 139; moral message in, 68
Gruss, Susanne, 32
Gunslinger (Dorn), 11, 13, 16, 79–91, 98–104, 139–40; Book I, 143n4, 145n5; Book II, 81, 145n5; capitalism in, 16, 79–104, 139–41; cultural narratives in, 16; "The Cycle," 81, 90–91, 102, 137–38; drugs in, 79–80, 102; fast food as a theme in, 86, 87; Homeric epithets in, 91, 137, 145n2, 146n14; the Horse, 79, 83–84, 91, 146n14; Hughes, 81–87, 89, 90, 95, 138–40, 145n8; Hughes as "cheeze" in a burger, 86–87, 91–92; Hughes as Christ, 87–88; Hughes as Janus, 88–89; Hughes as Lucky-Strike Green Man, 87; Hughes as Nobody, 89–90; Hughes as Robart, 16, 79–82, 86, 88, 90, 98, 102; Hughes as Rupert the Interior Decorator, 90–91; humor in, 98–100; "I" in, 95, 98, 145n5; identity as a theme in, 83–86; "The Interior Decorator Runs the Scenario of the Winged Car," 90; introduction, 102; Kool Everything, 83–84; Lil, 83, 145n8; longhorn in, 82–83; the Minotaur, 83; opening lines, 80;
political and cultural critiques in, 81; publication, 143n4; quest in, 79, 82–83; religion as a theme in, 86–88, 103; repetition in, 81; Slinger, 80, 82–84, 103, 139, 145n2, 145n5; "social investigation," 85; traditional formalist poetry in, 81
Gwynn, R. S., 12, 14–15, 35

Hacker, Marilyn, 11–15, 19–44, 45, 137, 141; disruptive nature of work, 27, 33; feminism, 20, 29, 143n2, 144n7; hedonism in work, 14, 19–44, 112; "lesbian ethics," 42; skaldic verse in, 145n3; themes of exile, 20; use of form, 27–28, 30–35, 45, 140. *See also individual works*
Hall, Radclyffe, 39
Hamby, Barbara, 4
Hammond, Karla, 34
Hardy, Donald, 117, 121
Hayes, Terrance, 12, 15, 64–66, 141
Hearts and Minds: Bodies, Poetry and Resistance in the Vietnam Era (Bibby), 10
hedonism: Aristippean, 22–23; attitudinal, 22–24; definition of, 22–23; Dionysian, 22–23, 43; Epicureanism, 22–23, 39–42; ethical systems of, 43; history of, 22; Intrinsic Attitudinal, 23–24; literary lineage, 24; morality and, 43; "new hedonism," 25
Herbert, William, 38–39
Hip Logic (Hayes), 64–66; anagrams in, 64–65, endnotes, 64; "A Gram of &s," 64; identity as a theme in, 66; masculinity as a theme in, 65–66
History and Class Consciousness (Lukacs), 47
Hoagland, Tony, 7
Hoffman, Abbie, 7
Hogue, Cynthia, 49

Homer, 95
Homeric epithets, 91, 93, 137
Houssaye, Arsene, 146n3
Howitt, Dennis, 56, 57
Howl and Other Poems (Ginsberg), 5
Hughes, Howard, 16, 79, 81–83; attempts to disguise himself, 83–84; germ phobias, 88–89, 145n10; reclusiveness, 88, 145n8; trip from Boston to Las Vegas, 81, 145n4
Hughes Tool Company, 89
"Human Universe" (Olson), 103
humanism, 127–28
humanist philosophy, 119–20
humor: destabilizing ideas through, 3; incongruent-resolution theory of, 33, 86; inversion as, 123; as an outlet of repression, 3; postmodern parody, 99–101; racial slurs/racism and, 56–57, 68; rebellious, 98–99; rhymes and, 52; role in poetry, 3–5, 9–11, 19, 147n1; sociopolitical critique, 5, 7, 9–10, 19, 138–39; theory, 13, 140–41; theory, "appropriate incongruity" of, 33, 37, 86–87; theory, linguistic, 13; theory, sociological, 13
Humor in Modern American Poetry (Trousdale), 5, 147n1; introduction, 5
Humor: International Journal of Humor Research (ed. Duhamel and Attardo), 4–5
Hutcheon, Linda, 99–101
"Hysteria" (Eliot), 146n2

Ignatow, David, 109
In Living Color, 7
Internal Resistance (Lockwood), 146n15
Intrinsic Attitudinal Hedonism, 23–24
intrinsic attitudinal pain, 23
intrinsic attitudinal pleasure, 23
intrinsic value of a life, 23–24; three key tenets of, 23
isomorphisms, 72

Jackson, Virginia, 8–9
Janus, 89
Jarman, Mark, 35
Jenkins, Grant, 82, 102, 104, 145nn8–10
Jenkins, Ron, 68
jokes: element of rebellion in, 3; engagement of incongruity in, 87; racist, 56–57

Keller, Lynn, 30, 35, 38
Kharms, Daniil, 118
King James Bible, 108
Kinnell, Galway, 10
Kirby, David, 4

La Presse, 146n3
Language writers, 49, 92, 144n6
Laughing and Ridicule: Towards a Social Critique of Humour (Billig), 99
"Laughter: An Essay on the Meaning of the Comic" (Bergson), 3, 123
Law & Order: Special Victims Unit, 67
"Letter to Menoeceus" (Epicurus), 41–42
Levertov, Denise, 108
Literary Wit (Michelson), 26
Lockwood, William J., 146n15
Logic of the Absurd, The (Palmer), 146n4
Love, Death, and the Changing of the Seasons (Hacker), 14–15, 19–44, 137; "Bloomingdale's I," 20, 143n1; "Dear Julie, here's your regular Sunday," 20; "Did you love well what very soon you left?," 43–44; "Eight Days in April," 40; food as

a theme in, 19–20; "Grand Hotel Malher," 19; "Having Kittens About Having Babies II," 27–28; "Having Kittens About Having Babies III," 24, 28–30; hedonism in, 14, 19–33, 36, 38, 40; humor in, 21, 37–38; "Lacoste IV," 19, 41; "Lesbian Ethics, or; Live Girl-Girl Sex Acts," 41; "March Wind," 41; Marie in, 39; moments of tension in, 37–38; "The Rape of the Lock," 140; Ray in, 30, 39–43; sexuality/homosexuality in, 14, 21, 27–30, 32–33, 37–43, 45, 140; societal norms confronted in, 21–22, 28, 31–33; sonnet form of, 27–28, 30–33, 36–38; "Substitute Teacher," 39; "Sweetheart, all day I've been listless and lame," 36–37; value system, 24; "Which didn't deter me from lying down," 37–39; "You, little one, are just the kind of boy," 43
Luck, Jessica Lewis, 48
Lukacs, Georg, 47
Lyric as Comedy: The Poetics of Abjection in Postwar America (McRae), 4, 64–65
lyric poetry, 4, 9, 16, 109

Manifest Destiny, 86–87
Marcuse, Herbert, 7
Marxism, 48
Mason, David, 35
McCaffery, Larry, 101
McCarthyism, 5, 85
McHale, Brian, 145n12
McHugh, Heather, 7
McMunn, Meradith T., 106, 123
McRae, Calista, 4, 64–65
"Meditating Formally" (Hacker), 33–34
Medusa, 107
Merwin, W. S., 10
"metafiction," 8

Metres, Philip, 6, 10–11
metrical poetry, 11
Michelson, Bruce, 26
Michelson, Peter, 27, 104
Miklitsch, Robert, 32
military industrial complex, 84–85, 91, 103
Mill, John Stuart, 76
Monroe, Jonathan, 109–10, 120
Monte, Steven, 110
Mother Goose, 113
Motte, Warren F., Jr., 52, 72
Mullen, Harryette, 11, 13, 15, 45–78, 79, 137, 139. *See also individual works*
Murphy, Eddie, 7
Muse & Drudge (Mullen), 55, 60

narrative poetry, 17
Native Son (Wright), 69
Nelson, Cary, 10
Nemerov, Howard, 3
"Neo-formalism: A Dangerous Nostalgia" (Sadoff), 35
New Critical Ideals, 5
New Formalist movement, 14, 35
Nielsen, Aldon Lynn, 49
9/11, 6–7, 11

"Ode on a Grecian Urn" (Keats), 92
Odyssey (Homer), 90
O'Hara, Frank, 7
Olson, Charles, 102–4
Omeros (Walcott), 16, 92–98; Achille, 93, 97–98; Afro-Caribbean identity in, 93–94, 97; Book 7, 95; capitalism in, 98; colonialism in, 96–98; Hector, 97–98; Herald Chastenet, 93; Homeric epithets in, 93–94, 137; "I" in, 95–98; Ma Kilman, 94; "Ma Rain," 94; Major Plunkett, 92–93; opening lines, 94; Philoctete, 94; Seven Seas/Omeros, 95–96; St.

Lucia in, 93, 95–98; terza rima form, 93; Winston James, 93
"On the Anagram and Its Functions" (Bares), 59
Oring, Elliott, 33, 37, 86–87, 140–41
Othello (Shakespeare), 140
Oulipian techniques, 13, 15, 47, 48, 50, 52, 75, 137; as a metaphor for oppression, 48–49; S + 7, 11, 71–72, 76
Oulipo (Ouvrior de Littérature Potentielle), 71–72, 144n1
Our Last First Poets (Nelson), 10
Oxford Dictionary of Modern Slang, 57
Oxford English Dictionary, 81–82, 89
Oxford English Dictionary Online, 46
Oxford Guide to Word Games, 46, 59

Palmer, Jerry, 146n4
parables, 112
Paris Spleen (Baudelaire), 108
Parisian Prowler, The (Baudelaire), 146n3
Perelman, Bob, 11
Perloff, Marjorie, 79–80, 102
Perseus, 107
Picture of Dorian Gray, The (Wilde), 25
Pleasure of the Feminist Text, The (Gruss), 32
Pleasure of the Text, The (Barthes), 31–32
Poems in Prose (Wilde), 108
poetry: abecedarian, 15, 52, 58; anagrams, 15, 46, 58–62; the blazon, 72–74; element of rebellion in, 3; epic, 9, 11, 13, 16, 79, 91; epistolary, 20; feminist, 14; genre conventions, 10, 12; lyric, 4, 16; lyricization of, negative consequences of, 9, 109; metrical, 11; narrative, 17; Oulipian, 11, 13, 47–48, 50, 137; procedural, 13, 15, 45–78; prose, 9, 12–13, 16–17, 105–35, 146n2; received forms, 14, 34, 35; role of humor in, 3–5, 9–11,

19; skaldic verse, 145n3; sonnets, 13–14, 19–44, 45; stand up, 4; terza rima, 93; traditional formalist, 81; Western, 16, 91; of witness, 10
"Portrait of Mr. W. H." (Wilde), 39
"Portrait of the Writer as a Fat Man" (Edson), 110–11, 122
posthumanism, 127, 130
"postmodern" fiction, 8
postmodern parody, 99–101
"Potential Literature" (Queneau), 72
"'Present, Infinitesimal, Infinite': The Political Vision and 'Femin' Poetics of Marilyn Hacker" (Biggs), 20, 28–29
procedural poetry, 13, 15, 45–78
prose poetry, 9, 12–13, 16–17, 105–35, 146n2; definition of, 109–11; history of, 108–9; issues of class and, 109–10; static predictability of, 111
Pryor, Richard, 7
Puns (Redfern), 52

Queneau, Raymond, 72

"Raven, The" (Poe), 92
Rebel Angels: 25 Poets of the New Formalism (ed. Jarman and Mason), 35; "Among Philistines" (Gwynn), 35–36
"Race and Ethnicity and Popular Humor" (Howitt and Owusu-Bempah), 56
Rainey, Ma, 94
Redfern, Robert, 52
reification, 15, 48, 49, 52–55, 77; definition of, 48; racism and, 15, 48, 57; sexism and, 15, 48
Reification, or the Anxiety of Late Capitalism (Bewes), 47–48, 63
rhymes: associative, 52; humor and, 52; slurs against marginalized peoples, 57

Rich, Adrienne, 10, 14, 35
Robbins, Amy Moorman, 74
Rock, Chris, 7
Roethke, Theodore, 10

Sadoff, Ira, 35
Saturday Night Live, 7
Seriously Funny (ed. Hamby and Kirby), 4
"Seven Words You Can Never Say on Television" (Carlin), 7
Shakespeare, William, 27, 38, 39, 71, 73, 140
Signifying Monkey, The (Gates), 144n4
Simpsons, The, 7
skaldic verse, 145n3
Sleeping with the Dictionary (Mullen), 11, 45–78, 79; abecedarians in, 15, 52, 58, 66; acrostics in, 15, 46; alliteration in, 53, 55; alphabetic structure of, 50–51; anagrams in, 15, 46, 58–66, 144n8; capitalism as a theme in, 15, 45, 47, 59, 62–63, 73, 75, 79, 141; clues in, 46; commodification of women as a theme in, 73–75; consumerism as a theme in, 53–54, 71–75; "Daisy Pearl," 45–46; "Dim Lady," 71, 73–74; "European Folktale Variant," 66–71, 76; fairy tales in, 66–71; formal constraints in work, 49, 50, 58, 77–78; Goldilocks in, 66–71; humor in, 49, 61–62, 75, 77; identity as a theme in, 60, 76, 144n6; "Jingle Jangle," 52–58, 75; language sounds in, 55–56; "The Lunar Lutheran," 58–59, 61–64; nonnarrative word play in, 15, 45, 51–52; objectification of women as a theme in, 54–55; Oulipian techniques in, 15, 47–50, 71–72, 76, 137; popular culture as a theme in, 62; prose poem "sonnets," 47; puns in, 46; reification in, 15, 48–49, 52–55, 77; religion as a theme in, 59, 62–64; rhyme in, 53–55; sex in, 45–46; slang in, 52–53; subjugation/discrimination as a theme in, 45, 47, 48–49, 66–68, 71, 79, 141; "Variation on a Theme Park," 71–72; violence in, 53, 55, 58, 63, 72–73; Walt Disney in, 72–73
social leveling, 56, 87–88
sonnet, 13–14, 19–45; conventions of, 14; history of, 14; patriarchal tradition of, 14; Shakespearean, 27
"Sonnet 116" (Shakespeare), 38–39
"Sonnet 130" (Shakespeare), 71, 73–74; closing lines, 73–74
South Park, 7
Spahr, Juliana, 49, 51
"speakerly" writing, 50, 144n4
speciesism, 17, 127–29
Stand Up Poetry (ed. Webb), 4
Stein, Gertrude, 49, 108
stereotype, racist, 57
Stewart, Jon, 7
Subversive Laughter (Jenkins), 68
Swift, Jonathan, 99

Tate, James, 7
Tender Buttons (Stein), 108
Tennyson, Alfred, 82
terza rima, 93
texts of bliss, 31–34
texts of pleasure, 31–34, 36–37
theory of "play," 7
"There Was an Old Woman," 112–13
Thomas, Lorenzo, 49
Three Stooges, The, 121
Tomlin, Lily, 7
Tormented Mirror, The (Edson), 116
Troubridge, Una, 39
Trousdale, Rachel, 5–6, 12, 143n1
Tunnel, The (Edson): anthropocentricism in, 121–22; "Ape and Coffee," 121–22; classification as a theme

in, 117–18; criticism of rationalism in, 120–21; humanism as a theme in, 131; "A Machine," 130–31; "Marionettes of Distant Masters," 124; "The Mountain Climber," 124–25; "My Head," 125–26; "The Philosophers," 120–21; "A Stone Is Nobody's," 122–23, 133; "The Way Things Are," 117–19

"Ulysses" (Tennyson), 82
University of Texas, 83
Upton, Lee, 115

Very Thing That Happens, The (Edson), 105–31; allegory in, 116; animal sacrifice in, 128–29; anthropocentric worldview in, 106–7; "Fables and Drawings," 106; fables in, 105–35; "The Fisherman and the Machine," 128–29; houses as a theme in, 115; humor in, 111–12, 114; illustrations in, 107, 119, 120, 146n6; introduction, 108; "The Neighborhood Dog," 114–16; "Of the Snake and the Horse," 105–7, 119; title page, 106; violence in, 106, 108; "The Wounded Breakfast," 112–14
Vietnam War, 5, 7, 10, 85; draft lotteries, 85
von Hallberg, Robert, 80

Walcott, Derek, 12, 16, 92–98, 141
Wallace, Ron, 4
Warner, Marina, 68
Webb, Charles Harper, 4
Westerns, 16, 91

"Who Reads Poetry?" (Jackson), 8–9
Wilde, Oscar, 24–26, 31, 38–39, 143n5; epigrams, 24–27, 31; hedonism, 27; indecency trial, 24, 29–30; prose poems, 108, 112
With Strings (Bernstein), 75; capitalism as a theme in, 75–76; epigraph, 75–76; hedonistic ethics in, 76; identity as a theme in, 76–77; "log rhythms," 76; "Notes and Acknowledgments," 77; Oulipian techniques, 75
Wolfe, Cary, 127, 128, 129, 130, 132
Women's Liberation movement, 10
World War II, 5, 7, 11, 108
Wright, Richard, 69
Writer in Politics, The (Forche), 10
"writerly" language, 50, 144n4

Young, Dean, 7

Zawacki, Andrew, 109, 111, 146n3

About the Author

Photo credit: Maureen Drennan

Carrie Conners is a professor of English at LaGuardia CC-CUNY. She is the author of two poetry collections. Her debut collection, *Luscious Struggle* (BrickHouse Books 2019), was selected as a 2020 Paterson Poetry Prize Finalist. Her second collection, *Species of Least Concern*, is forthcoming from Main Street Rag Publishing (2022, expected). Her essays and poems have appeared in the *Journal of Working-Class Studies*, *Bodega*, *Kestrel*, *Quiddity*, *RHINO*, and *Chautauqua*, among other publications.

www.ingramcontent.com/pod-product-compliance
Lightning Source LLC
Chambersburg PA
CBHW030625230426
43661CB00053B/2148